I0160715

About the Author

John Weir, BCH, CI
Hypnosis Center for Motivation and Habit Management,
Munhall, PA

John Weir is the creator of the *Mental Caddie* golf improvement program and has helped countless people take their golf game to the next level. He has worked with many athletes in his private practice including a Pennsylvania athlete of the year who was a 16-year-old golfer.

Known in Pittsburgh as the area's Smoke Cessation Specialist as well as a Peak Performance Coach, his work has been featured in all media forums. He is also a regular columnist for the *Journal of Hypnotism* and has produced over 20 hypnosis CD programs.

John was awarded the Charles Tebbetts trophy in 2008 at the annual National Guild of Hypnotists Convention.

Dedication

This book is dedicated to my amazing parents who have unconditionally supported all my endeavors. I am eternally grateful for all your love and support throughout my career, especially through all the tough times.

Mom, I want to thank you for your never-ending support, optimism, and prayers. Your loving words of encouragement have given me the belief that I can achieve anything. Thank you for being my cheerleader, my confidence booster, and the absolute best mom a young entrepreneur could ask for.

Dad, I want to thank you for all the priceless guidance you have given me from day one. Thank you for listening to all of my ideas and putting up with my endless phone calls . . . you truly have the patience of a saint. Dad you are the best father a son could ask for. Thank you so much for always being there for me. I could have never accomplished this if it wasn't for you.

I want to thank Sara Harenchar for copy editing this book.

FORWARD

We have been fortunate through the years to publish authors who have a deep love and enthusiasm for the art, science, and philosophy of our profession—the practice of hypnotism.

John Weir is another shining star in our NGH galaxy of authors. He loves his chosen profession and is filled with excited enthusiasm about how hypnosis can help people. He has "been there" and "done that" when it comes to building a practice as a consulting hypnotist, and now shares it all in this valuable book.

We have always said that in order to sell something you have to *own* it, and hypnotism is no different. John *owns* it and so can *you* if you study this book, feel John's enthusiasm and put the information to work in your own practice.

Dr. Dwight F. Damon, President
National Guild of Hypnotists, Inc.

CONTENTS

Dedication

Foreward

© 2010 - National Guild of Hypnotists, Inc.
All rights reserved
Lightning Source Publishing
ISBN: 978-1-885846-16-7
Printed in the United States

CHAPTER 1
THE JOURNEY BEGINS

Since I was 19 years old I have been selling something invisible: I have been selling hypnosis. When I first became a hypnotist, one question constantly plagued my thoughts, "How do you sell something both intangible and unconventional?" I quickly learned that in order to build a successful career in hypnosis, you must learn to sell yourself and your services. I noticed that the technique of "selling" hypnosis is something often ignored. This book was written to help new hypnotists minimize the learning curve in regards to selling their new skills, so they can begin making money in this profession right away. In the pages to follow, you will find a straightforward guide to selling hypnosis. You will learn effective strategies that when applied will immediately increase your hypnosis sales, business, and income.

If you think about it, sales and hypnosis are very closely related. First of all, there is an extensive amount of material written on both subjects, and it would impossible to attempt to put every technique about both hypnosis and sales into a single book. This book is designed to be a quick start guide to selling. The primary goal of this book is to provide you with a basic foundation in the world of sales. What makes this book unique is that it is focused entirely on selling hypnosis; all examples are directly related to this profession.

The secondary goal of this book is to pique your interest in the art of selling. It is my intention to get you so excited about sales that this book will be the first of many on this fascinating and vital subject. For those who have read sales books before, let me praise you for your commitment to personal growth and development. I know this book will inspire many new ideas, and at the very least remind you of effective techniques to bring back into your daily sales routine.

One could easily make the argument that hypnosis is selling and selling is hypnosis. Wouldn't you agree that really persuasive salespeople are in a way skillful hypnotists? Great salespeople have the uncanny way of utilizing waking hypnotic states to tantalize our senses, emotionally hook us to their products, and magically get us to say yes (sometimes in spite of our better judgment). Rather than selling a product, we sell our clients' subconscious minds on the idea of adopting new positive behaviors, attitudes, and mindsets. Another great benefit you will receive as a result of learning the art of selling is how you can utilize sales techniques in your sessions. As you read this book, think about how you can use these techniques to help elicit changes in your clients, as well as how you can use what you do during your sessions for the process of selling.

Finally and most importantly, sales and hypnosis are closely related because both have concepts that are theoretical and concepts that are practical. Even though this is a quick start guide, the information found in this book works in the real world and not just in theory. Since 2001 I have been earning my living as a hypnotist, and a hypnotist only. There are many successful hypnotists who only work part time in the profession and supplement their income with other work. There is nothing wrong with this decision, but hypnotists who have supplemental incomes don't depend upon hypnosis to pay the bills and put food on the table the way I do. The techniques found in this book come from my real world experiences of selling hypnosis, and growing my business from the ground up.

What you are about to read are simple sales strategies that will help your business prosper. You will learn how to easily overcome common objections, how to sell the value of your services, and effective ways to close the sale. This book will teach you what to do on the phone when clients call, how to categorize the caller, and how to track your success on the phone. You will also discover techniques for creating rapport, building relationships, and closing face to face sales. Now let's get started into the hypnotic world of sales!

CHAPTER 2
TWO THINGS YOU MUST KNOW!

Before going any farther, there are two profound truths that you need to know and understand about this profession. If you want to succeed as a hypnotist, it is essential that you live by these truths.

Truth Number 1: In this profession you have two roles; the helper and the entrepreneur.

Now that you are a hypnotist, it's important to know that you will always have two roles to fulfill in order to succeed. The first role is the helper. Since you are a hypnotist, I would make the assumption that you genuinely want to help people succeed at reaching their goals. Helping people reach their goals is your primary role in this profession, and you will find that helping people produce successful results is one of the easiest ways to grow your business.

The helper role is obvious, but the role that is often forgotten yet is equally important is the role of the entrepreneur. You are now in business for yourself, and in order for your practice to grow you must begin to act like an entrepreneur. It is important to educate yourself about business just like you educate yourself about hypnotism. In the same way it is your task to help your clients succeed, and it is your responsibility to grow your practice because your efforts will determine your level of success.

These two roles are vital to your success whether you want to be a full-time practitioner or not. Understand that if you are a good hypnotist but know nothing about business you will never make it in the long run. The opposite is also true. If you are great in business but an ineffective hypnotist you won't be in this business very long. For your practice to prosper, you need to educate yourself in both of these areas because the more effort you put into learning, the more you will succeed!

There is one very easy way to learn about selling and running a business, and that is to use your idle time in the car listening to audio programs. When I started my business at 19 years old, I didn't have a MBA or even a college credit in business. I got my education driving around in my car listening to selling experts like Zig Zigler and Tom Hopkins, as well as outstanding motivators like Tony Robbins and Les Brown. I would strongly suggest listening to everything you can get your hands on, and using your car as your university. You will be amazed by how quickly you will learn and how much information can be absorbed in this way.

Truth Number 2: You are allowed to make a lot of money in a helping profession.

As a veteran of hypnotism conventions and after having talked with many other hypnotists, I have found that there are some people that feel guilty about making money for their services because they are in a helping profession. I want to clear up this misconception right now and let you know that it's ok to make a lot of money helping people and it is also ok to charge what you are worth.

Unless you have taken a vow of poverty or are in a religious vocation, it's perfectly acceptable to produce a high income from helping people succeed. Doctors help people every day and they also make more money than the average person. Do you think that doctors feel guilty about making a lucrative income because they are helping people? Of course not, and neither should you. Hypnotherapy is a valuable, life-changing service and hypnotists that produce results deserve to be compensated with a high income. Take a moment to think about what you help people achieve with hypnosis. For example: you don't just help a person stop smoking, but you also have a hand in saving their life. Your services have saved this person thousands of dollars, helped to prevent painful and irreversible diseases as well as greatly improved the quality of their life. What are these things worth? Some would consider those three advantages to be priceless commodities, especially to the person who suffers the consequences. You offer an extremely powerful service that helps to transform lives, so it is ok to be financially compensated for your services.

Another misconception that needs to be clarified is the idea that because you are in a helping profession you need to charge next to nothing for your service. Unless you are focusing on volume through group sessions, charging next to nothing hurts your business for several reasons. First of all, some people think that the more expensive something is, the better it is. For example, if you had to get brain surgery would you shop around to find the cheapest brain surgeon or would you find the best regardless of cost? Would you ever want the cheapest electrician to rewire your house or someone you know will get the job done right? Do you think people want to go the cheapest hypnotist? The answer is no. They want to go to a hypnotist that can create the results they are looking for in their life. When you learn to sell the value of your service, a client will pay you whatever you are requesting.

Next, if you charge what your services are worth and don't undersell yourself, your clients will have more success in their sessions. There are only two types of investments a person makes; an investment of time (energy) and an investment of money. Your goal is to get your clients to invest in both ways, because by doing so you will create greater success in your office. When a client invests money into your services, they come into your office more motivated and committed to a successful outcome. Isn't that true in your own life? When you have invested your time and money into something aren't you more committed to getting something good out of the experience? Our job as hypnotists is to create change in a person's life. Getting a person to make a financial investment is an element that aids in the change process. You will know that every client walking through your door is committed to and ready for success. Charging what you are worth is a win-win for all involved.

One last thought: when you are making a lot of money, you are helping a lot of people. Your business can't be growing unless you are producing successful results. Success breeds more success, and as you help your clients succeed in their lives, they help you succeed financially. With every client success story, you are increasing your ability to be a positive influence with more people. Know with confidence that it is ok to make a lucrative income helping people succeed.

CHAPTER 3
THE SALE STARTS WITH YOU

All sales start with you. What exactly does that mean? It means that the first thing a person will buy is you. Your first job is to sell the people around you on the idea that you are a person who can help them create the success they desire in life. It is important that you get your potential clients to feel confident in you, and the best way to achieve this feat is by living with congruity. Congruity is a term used in NLP or Neuro-Linguistic Programming that simply means walking your talk. There are several different ways a person can live with congruity, and this chapter will examine these ways so that you can create more confidence and charisma when selling your services.

The first way a person projects congruity is by having all levels of communication send off the same message. It is important to know that the communication process is made up of more than just words. We communicate on three distinct levels: non-verbal communication, vocal tonalities, and words. When most hypnotists get started in this business, they are often overly concerned with finding all the right words to say to a client. Even though words are an extremely potent force they make up only a small percentage of the communication process. If you were to break down communication into percentages then 55% of communication is non-verbal, 38% is vocal tonalities (how we use our voice), and only 7% is the words we use. Communication consists of non-verbal cues and signals given off through body language, as well as how we use our voices through our tones, inflictions, and volume. You must be aware that more is said through the way we use our bodies and the way we communicate our message with our voices than simply saying the right words. It is vitally important to understand the communication breakdown, because your ability to communicate effectively will determine the level of success you will achieve. Hypnotist Marshall Sylver said "Communication equals wealth." As you read on, you will learn how to utilize this information to increase your sales and your success with your clients.

So how does this relate back to congruity and the idea that all sales start with you? Simply put, congruity happens when all of these levels of communication match; your body language, your tonality of voice and your choice of words are all delivering the same message. The more congruity all your levels of communication have, the more confidence and belief a person will have in you. When you communicate with congruity, you radiate trust to your potential clients and it sends the message that you have the ability to help them. Congruity always makes it much easier for people not only to say yes to you but to really want to say yes to your requests because everything about you makes them feel comfortable. The opposite is also true and must be avoided. If you communicate with incongruity, you can make a person feel uncomfortable and unreceptive to your ideas.

Let me provide you with a brief example of a person who projects incongruity. Take a moment to think of a person who is visibly upset, and we know this because of her body language. She is standing with her arms crossed, her breathing rate is very short and fast, and her face is all red with a scowl across her lips. Now, imagine you are a concerned friend and you want to see if you can do anything to help her. You walk up to her, ask her if anything is wrong, and she snaps back with a sharp, "Nothing. Nothing is wrong." Do you believe her answer? Of course not. So why don't we believe her? It's because there is incongruity on one of the communication levels and in this case it occurred because the words didn't match her body language. When a person tries to communicate or sell with incongruity, it can make the other person feel suspicious, uneasy, or cautious. If incongruity occurs when you are selling hypnosis or working with your clients, it becomes very difficult to sell or succeed in session due to the importance of trust and rapport in our work.

Make sure that when you communicate, you have congruity at all times, especially when selling your services. The way you do this is by standing with good posture with your head held high, and looking your clients in the eye. When you speak, do so with a confident and self assured tone in your voice. Finally, avoid using weak words like if, hope, and try. Choose words that convey a confident and positive message. Use stronger words like when you succeed, I know you will enjoy this, you can do it.

Your potential clients want you to be confident in your services and your ability to help them. If you don't feel particularly confident in yourself, have no fear. There is an easy way to project confidence to all you communicate with. The way you do it is by "Acting as if . . ." It's that simple. If you don't feel confident, simply act as if you were. In order to do this, you must first do a fun activity.

ACTIVITY: Find a room where you can be alone and pretend that you are a world famous actor who can play any role. Imagine that you have to play the role of a confident salesperson and begin by standing in the way this character would. What posture would they have? What would they do with their arms? How do they hold their head? How do they look at people? It can help to do this in front of a mirror so that you can make sure this behavior projects confidence.

Next, begin to walk around the room as this character. How would a confident salesperson move? What do they do with their body as they walk around and move about the room? What type of gestures do they make that project confidence? How do they use their hands? Spend 5 minutes walking around the room as this character. Have fun with this activity.

Now that you know how this confident salesperson uses their body, the next thing an actor would experiment with is how to use their voice to play this role. All actors take the time to play around with the tonality of their voices so that they truly project this character to their audience. Spend a few minutes pretending you are talking to a client, and acting as if you were a confident salesperson. How does this person sound? How quickly do they speak? What type of inflections do they have in their voice? Speak like that character for a few minutes.

Finally, learn the word choice of this character. Take some time delivering sales pitches as this dynamic salesperson. Think about the words you are now going to use to sell your services. Spend a few minutes acting out this person's behaviors. Notice the way you feel when you act as if you were an effective and confident salesperson.

Now that you know how to play this role, go out there and act as if you are this person and watch your sales skyrocket! After you act out this role for awhile you will simultaneously develop real confidence in yourself and your services. As you project this level of congruity, your potential clients will feel comfortable and believe the message you are delivering. They will also get the feeling that you are a person that can get the job done.

The other way to possess congruity is through leading by example. Remember, all sales start with you, and the first thing people will buy is you. In order to successfully sell hypnosis, you must believe wholeheartedly in the benefits, success, and empowerment it can create in a person's life. You also must truly believe that you can help a person, not only to change his or her, but do it in an efficient and effective way. The fastest way to develop an unwavering belief in the process of hypnosis is to use hypnosis in your own life to achieve your goals. This practice will validate the effectiveness of hypnosis to you on the deepest levels so that you can sell it with conviction and confidence. When talking with potential clients, I always tell them that I used hypnosis to become a non-smoker in just one session, to have 4 wisdom teeth removed without anesthesia, and I also explain how I use it to improve my golf game. These examples demonstrate to potential clients that I use hypnosis in my own life, which in turn strengthens the client's confidence in me as a hypnotist. Giving examples from my own life has also helped to solidify in my mind that hypnosis is very effective, and if it can help me, I know it could help others.

It is my fundamental belief that hypnotism is more a philosophy for living rather than just a profession, and I feel that it is important to live your life in a healthy, loving, and optimistic way. I'm sure that you have heard the expression "actions speak louder than words," and this type of congruity could simply be called "walking your talk."

This type of congruity creates confidence in yourself, in the process, and in the minds of your potential clients. Again, the sale starts with you and people will buy you. If you live life with a positive, happy, and upbeat attitude, people will want what you have. When you can show them how easy it is to change with hypnosis by using it yourself, they will want to follow your example.

Congruity is a powerful tool that will increase your sales and success. However, please keep in mind that nobody is perfect and to have an expectation of perfection will definitely lead to unhappiness. The more you can live your life with congruity, the better, however keep in mind that you don't have to know how to lay an egg to cook one. This means you don't have to be depressed or have been depressed in the past to help someone overcome the negative feelings of depression, nor do you need to be a professional athlete to help professionals improve their skills. The purpose of this chapter is just to remind you that people will be watching you and looking to you as a leader now that you are a hypnotist. So if there are some things you can do to have more congruity in your life, maybe like become healthier or more positive, do it and watch your success in what you do rise to new levels.

CHAPTER 4
RAPPORT: THE ESSENTIAL ELEMENT

Rapport is an essential element in both selling and hypnosis. Rapport can be described as a feeling of trust, connection, or harmony with another person. By learning how to quickly establish rapport with potential clients, you will make it easier to successfully close them on your services. A very important thing to know about rapport is that rapport is not a static state which once achieved is everlasting. Rapport is a process that needs to be established, maintained, and then nurtured continuously in order to strengthen the bond of trust.

The techniques you are about to read are very simple, yet they are extremely effective ways to instantly create rapport with your potential clients and anybody else you wish to persuade. There is a wealth of material on the subject of rapport building so this book will only briefly cover these techniques. The techniques covered in this chapter do work, and have helped me since I started practicing hypnosis when I was 19-years-old. Even as a young practitioner, I used to these techniques to make people feel comfortable with me in my clinical practice, as well as to help sell myself to others. As you apply these simple techniques to your life, you will be absolutely amazed with your results.

The easiest way to gain rapport with another person is to find commonalities between the two of you. When you are speaking to potential clients, imagine you are a detective and it is your job to find something that you both have in common. If the person is wearing a golf shirt, you could ask them if they play golf. The potential client may have a fancy watch or a unique piece of jewelry on that you could ask about, and you can then find out how they came into possession of such a beautiful thing. Become a detective and find some common ground that the two of you share. This practice gets a person to start talking, opening up, and most importantly, feeling comfortable with you. Common ways to connect with people include: their hometown, size of family, kids, sports, hobbies, clothing, their business, department store sales, new trends, music, cell phones, computers, and anything else that you share in common with that person. Just one common interest or experience is really all that is needed to break the ice and begin the rapport building process. It is important to remember these common interest points, because in future conversations it is an easy lead-in to avoid any awkward encounters. Always remember: the absolute easiest way to create rapport is to find common ground with the other person.

As mentioned in the previous chapter, there are three levels of communication: non-verbal, vocal tonalities, and words. Since non-verbal communication is the most powerful form of communication, it would only make sense to start with techniques which elicit rapport non-verbally. These techniques are very effective in face to face selling situations, negotiations, as well as working with clients in your office. The techniques most commonly used by hypnotists, NLP practitioners, and great salespeople to elicit rapport non-verbally are called mirroring, matching, and cross-matching.

Matching is slyly and very discretely imitating another person's behavior. Please understand that this imitation is not done in a mimicking or mocking manner. When you are matching a person's movements, you must do so in a very subtle way that is intended for the subconscious mind.

Here are several oversimplified examples of matching: If your potential client scratches his face with his right hand, then in a similar fashion you scratch your face with your right hand. If your potential client sits with his arms crossed, then you sit with your arms crossed in a similar way. If the potential client crosses his left leg, then you would match his movement and posture by crossing your left leg.

Mirroring is the same thing as matching, but instead of matching the behavior exactly, you do the opposite. This exercise gives the subconscious mind the illusion that they are staring at themselves in the mirror. When mirroring and sitting across from someone, if the person scratches her face with her right hand, then you would scratch your face with your left hand. If a person is sitting there with her left leg crossed then you cross your right. It really is that simple.

Cross-Matching is matching a person's repetitive behavior with a similar one. For example, if the potential client keeps tapping his foot, then you can tap your pencil at the same pace.

Your ultimate goal with these techniques is to subtly resemble the other person's body postures, positions, and gestures.

Here are a few important things to know when mirroring and matching potential clients. *First*, when matching gestures and movements, you have a 10-15 second window to do a similar gesture. This is an important rule to follow because if you do everything at the exact same time as they do, then the person will think you are mimicking them and all rapport is lost. *Second*, you don't have to do exactly what the other person does. For example, if your potential client scratches the top of their head, rather than do that, you might rub your nose or maybe scratch your cheek. You just want to do something that resembles the behavior. *Lastly*, it is very important to know that it isn't necessary to mirror and match 100% of the person's actions, you only have to use these techniques with 60 -70% of the person's major movements and gestures.

These techniques may seem too simple to work at first, yet they are extremely powerful because they affect people on an unconscious level. You may be asking yourself right about now, "why is this important and how does it create rapport with people?" The reason these techniques are so powerful is because they are based on the law of attraction which tells us that "like attracts like". By subtly matching a person's behavior, we send the message to their subconscious mind that "I like this person and can trust them because they are just like me!" In life we gravitate toward people we are most like, and when you utilize mirroring and matching, people will feel an instant connection with you. This rapport is very important in the selling process, and usually is just the thing to get a person to say yes to your requests. When you learn to master these techniques, there isn't anybody in the world that will be able to resist your persuasive power.

Now that you know what mirroring, matching, and cross-matching are, it is time to discover how to use these techniques to persuade a person through a process called pacing and leading. When you are matching and mirroring a person's body posture and several of their behaviors, you are actually pacing them. Global NLP Training defines pacing as a method used by communicators to quickly establish rapport by matching certain aspects of their behavior to those with whom they are communicating. Some common gestures and movements that are good to pace include: a person's breathing rate, repetitive movement (like a foot tap), head movements, a person's blinking rate, body sways, hand gestures, and so on.

Once you have been pacing a person for a short period of time, if you are in rapport with the person, you can begin to lead their behavior. When you pace a person, you are entering into their map of the world to create rapport with them. After you have rapport, you job is to bring the person into your map of the world so persuasion can take place. You achieve this by making a gesture or a movement that is different than the way they have been behaving while watching to see if the person does something similar, as if they were pacing you. For example, imagine the client is sitting there with their hands on their lap. If you have rapport and suddenly scratch the top of your head then the client will follow your lead and behave in a similar fashion as you did. This process is called leading, and it is a covert way of testing your rapport with someone as well as a way of manipulating a person's behavior and actions. This technique is very important when selling your services. If you notice that you have successfully paced someone, obtained rapport, and you are now leading their behavior, then it is time to go in for the close.

Pacing and leading are also very useful in getting a person who is demonstrating resistant behaviors to open up. Resistant behaviors include: sitting with arms folded, legs crossed, and other closed body language. By mirroring and matching potential clients' body posture, pacing their movements such as breathing patterns and arm gestures, you can slowly begin opening up your body posture to reflect more open and receptive body language.In turn, the person will gradually begin opening up to follow your lead. This will help to put them into a more receptive mindset about your services or the session.

In the real world, pacing and leading are always occurring naturally. For example, have you ever been around a group of smokers and as soon as one person lights up, everybody does the same thing? The next time you see a new mother rocking her baby around some friends, you will notice everyone around her swaying too. Next time you are eating at a restaurant, do some people watching and notice the people who are in good rapport and who are not. You will recognize it right away knowing what you know now. A group that is in very close rapport is often easy to notice because when one takes a drink, within a second or two, the others at the table will take a drink. Finally, have you ever noticed in a business meeting that as soon as one person stands up, all those in rapport follow right along? Now that you are aware of it, you will notice this happening everywhere. As you master these skills you will be amazed at the vast increase in your ability to get people to say yes to your requests.

Besides mirroring and matching the non-verbal communication patterns of your potential client, you can also elicit subconscious rapport by making adjustments in your vocal tonality to match theirs. The rules of mirroring and matching also apply to the way a person speaks, and there are many elements that you can match to make a person feel very comfortable with you, so that they will be more receptive to your message. Things that you will want to pay attention to include: The rate of speech (speed), the volume, the pitch, the tone, different inflections, the tempo, and the cadence. The more you can match another person's vocal characteristics, the more rapport you will gain with this person.

In my opinion, the rate and volume are the two most essential elements to match, and failure to do so can quickly break rapport. I learned this lesson during the most valuable business training I have ever experienced: working as a telemarketer. Telemarketing taught me many priceless lessons, including how to overcome rejection and how to achieve a set goal. Most importantly, telemarketing clearly demonstrated to me the value of matching a person's voice to make the persuasion process much more effective. I didn't learn this lesson through achieving tremendous success. I learned this lesson after hours and hours of failed calls and much frustration due to my lack of sales. At the time, I was a teenager living in Southwestern Pennsylvania, and if you have ever been to this part of Pennsylvania before, you know it's a mixture between city and country. We have big cities like Pittsburgh, but we also have farmland just a few minutes outside of the city. I am definitely more of a city person and I tend to think, act, and especially speak faster than some of the easier going people in the rural areas. After a few weeks of telemarketing and not achieving the success I desired, I started to evaluate my performance on the job to figure out the flaw that was preventing me from getting more sales. I had a hard time pinpointing what the problem was, since I had internalized my phone script, knew great responses to objections, and knew my product inside out. I just couldn't figure out what it was and why some days I had great success and others I had nothing but rejection. Then it hit me during one successful day at work: it wasn't the words I was using that were preventing my success, but it was the area. That particular day, I was calling on people in the city, people that communicated faster and liked material presented to them in a more rapid fashion compared to people living outside of the city. I asked my supervisor where most of my sales came from and he reported back to me that ALL of my sales came from calling on the city. Driving home that night, my mind was restlessly trying to figure out why I was more successful in the city, but I never came up with an answer until the next day at work when I had to call on a rural part of Pennsylvania. After a few calls, I finally discovered the answer completely by accident. I called a gentleman who was talking very slowly. I started my sales pitch and I couldn't even get a few words out before he stopped me and said "I don't want what you're selling…I can't stand you fast talking city slickers bothering me all the time. Stop calling me!" (Click) Normally, I would have laughed and went on to the next number to go at it again. Instead, I had a revelation. His comment made me realize what the problem was: I was talking too fast to connect with people in the rural areas. This one conversation helped me to get my first sale in the farmlands of Pennsylvania that day, as well as opened the door to many more sales by making this adjustment in my rate of speech.

Do not underestimate the importance of matching your potential client's rate of speech because this truly is a rapport builder or destroyer. For example, I have the great pleasure of meeting people from all around the world. My friends from down south are some of the nicest people I have ever met and can sometimes be very slow talkers. If they are speaking to me in a slow and lulling tone, often times they start to lose me. My fast moving mind begins to wander, and I find myself drifting in and out of the conversation. If you are a slow talker, this is quite alright. Just understand that when you are talking to someone who lives at a high pace, you must make the conscious effort to speed up your rate of speech. The opposite is also true if you are a fast talker. If you are rambling off ideas and thoughts in the typical rapid fashion, but conversing with a slow talker, you will definitely lose them due to information overload. Your job is to slow down and take your time communicating your message so that it can be processed by your client.

Finally, you can be a much more persuasive salesperson and hypnotist if you learn to speak your client's language. People experience the world through 3 primary modalities which are auditory, visual, and kinesthetic. When people speak, they express themselves in ways that reveal their primary modality. For example, a visual person might say "I sure like the looks of the new project," an auditory person might say "starting this new project is music to my ears," and finally, a kinesthetic person might say "I have such a great feeling about this new project." Why is this valuable to know when selling your services or working with your clients? Because when you speak to clients in ways they best understand, they are more likely to comply with your requests. It gives them a feeling of rapport and the sense that you know exactly what they want since you are communicating to them on their level. Train yourself to be an active listener. Everybody will reveal their dominate modality as they communicate and all you have to do is pay attention to the words they select to express themselves with. Then begin adjusting your language to match theirs. Modality is very easy to pick up on, and recognizing it in a potential client will boost your sales as well as your effectiveness with your clients. Here is a list of words commonly used by each modality. Remember these words so that you can hear them in conversation and use them to create rapport.

VISUAL WORDS: Look, see, gaze, glare, view, picture, visualize, focus, perceive, appear, stare, glance, bright, dim, shiny, brilliant, vivid, watch, observe, show, envision, vision, sight, project, and scene.

EXPRESSIONS: You look great today, these are some bright prospects, I have a grand vision of the future, let me glance this over, let me have a closer look, show me the money, it appears we are moving in the right direction, I can vividly envision my success, that guy glared at me, I have a brilliant idea, come here and watch this . . .

KINESTHETIC WORDS: Feel, touch, grasp, absorb, process, internalize, grab, hit, smooth, sharp, dull, hot, cold, clumsy, tight, loose, concrete, rub, sense, experience, suffer, undergo, handle, contact, and hold.

EXPRESSIONS: This gives me a good feeling inside, let me process this information, that hypnotist sure is a smooth talker, I'm feeling hot tonight, I can't quite grasp the concept, get a handle on things, that guy rubs me the wrong way, get a hold on things, once I absorb this I know I will remember it, I have suffered with this long enough, I must undergo a treatment, this is a concrete idea . . .

AUDITORY WORDS: Hear, talk, sound, tune, harmony, rhythm, loud, noisy, quiet, tell, inquire, say, express, call, recall, speak, whine, ring, silence, thunderous, echo, resonance, listen, ask, and mention.

EXPRESSIONS: Sounds good to me, that's music to my ears, I'm in tune today, I can't recall our last session, I received a thunderous applause, listen up, I hear what you are saying, I'm calling to inquire about your services, there was a feeling of harmony at the party, that resonates with me, I'm sometimes a whiny person, that rings true, let me hear it once more, the concert was sure noisy . . .

These lists could go on forever, but now with this awareness you will be able to pinpoint your clients' modality within minutes. Make sure to reuse common phrases used by your clients in the persuasion process in order to increase your success.

Let me give you a brief summary of this chapter. Rapport is a feeling of trust, connection, and harmony between two people. Building rapport is a process, not a constant state, so make sure to use techniques both to gain and sustain it. The easiest way to build rapport is to find common ground with your client. Connect with them by asking about their family, interests, work, and so on. Next, you learned that we communicate in three different ways. We communicate with our body language, our tonality of voice, and the words we use. You learned about how to build rapport on all three levels through mirroring and matching, pacing and leading, adjusting tonality, and speaking the clients' language. Now it's time to put all of them into action. After utilizing these techniques for a short time, you will find yourself naturally doing so with everyone you meet, and becoming more persuasive then you can imagine. I want to finish this chapter with one final warning. Make sure you never blatantly mimic someone, or else you will destroy all rapport with that client, and chances are you will never gain it back. Please be sure to never do this in a joking way or in a way that makes fun of the other person. Finally, never imitate a person's accent. If you imitate an accent, you will always be perceived as rude and disrespectful. Remember, these techniques are designed to elicit unconscious rapport, so it is your job to do this in a discrete way. Have fun with these techniques, and most importantly, use them to help you succeed in life.

CHAPTER 5
THE PHONE CALL

In this profession, most of your sales opportunities will come from incoming phone calls from potential clients. It is essential to understand the proper way to handle phone calls so that your practice can begin growing. This chapter is going to breakdown the elements of the phone call, including: effective ways to answer the telephone, the importance of getting clients to invest their time, how to classify the caller, and the ultimate goal of every incoming phone call.

Before going on, it's worth mentioning that when you are talking to clients on the phone the same rules of rapport building apply, with one exception. Since the client is unable to see you, the communication ratio changes and vocal tonality (rate, volume, etc.), not non-verbal communication, becomes the most powerful level of communication. This is also true in your hypnosis sessions. In his book, *Mind Bending for Mind Mending Brain,* Green said that when a person is hypnotized, communication is 90% vocal tonalities and 10% words. It is my opinion that this percentage would be closer to 70% when talking on the phone compared to hypnosis, but regardless what the exact percentage is, it is essential to keep this in mind while selling on the phone.

The first thing that needs to be done before answering any phone call is to put a big smile on your face and get yourself feeling excited. When you answer your phone with a smile on your face and with an attitude of excitement it will be projected through your voice. You want to treat this caller as if you have been waiting to talk to them all your life, and now it's finally your chance. This doesn't mean being overwhelming or sounding desperate for a client, but a subtle enthusiasm to talk to this person. When you answer the phone in this way, your client will immediately get the sense that you are a person they would like to work with. Answering the call with a smile is so simple, yet so many people don't do it and end up giving off a feeling off disconnection or lack of interest. I can't stress enough how important smiling on the phone is. During my telemarketing experience, they posted the word smile in our cubicle and gave everyone a mirror to make sure we were always smiling when making calls. Just remember Smiles Equal Sales.

A common question often arises at my training courses is "what is the best way to answer your phone?" Believe it or not, the way you answer your phone will play a major role in booking the client or losing the sale. The way you answer your phone is important because many of your potential clients will open the phone book or find a directory online and begin going down the list calling on every hypnotist, hoping to find the right one. Many ineffective businesspeople take for granted the importance of this initial contact, and can end up missing out on tens of thousands of dollars in potential business. Be sure to plan your opening line so that you can utilize it for your success.

So, what is the proper way to answer your incoming calls? Let me answer this question by starting with what NOT to do. First, never answer your phone generically by just stating your name or your practice name. This will immediately create a disconnection because it doesn't make the client feel welcome, and strongly implies that you are too busy for them. Next, many hypnotists work out of their home, which is perfectly acceptable. However, make sure you have a way to discern the difference between personal calls and business calls. It is very unprofessional to have kids answering a business call and then calling for mom or dad to answer the phone. One way to get around this is to get a distinctive ring setup with your phone company. This enables you to have two numbers on the same phone line with two distinct rings so you can identify which number is being called. If you are at home and a business call comes in, make sure that you answer it in a quiet place where there are no kids running around or televisions making lots of noise. Always remember that this initial contact will provide your caller with an impression. It is your job to make sure it's a good one.

The purpose of your opening line is to make a connection with your client by making them feel welcomed and important. It's my opinion that all calls should be started with a powerful presupposition. Presuppositions are nothing more than basic assumptions that can be used to covertly deliver ideas or suggestions to your client. If you use your opening line effectively, then you get the persuasion process started right away. I sometimes think of my opener as having two parts, a starter and a leading statement.

In my opinion, one of the best ways to start your opener is by thanking the person for calling your office. This is a great starter because it indirectly tells the caller that you appreciate them and their business, which subtly boosts their ego by making them feel important. A suggested way to begin your opening line would be "Thank you for choosing (*your practice name)*, my name is Mr. Jones . . ." Even though this simple starter is a little generic, it is very effective. The powerful word in this starter is the word choosing because this word presupposes that they have already chosen your practice simply by making the phone call. By thanking them for choosing you, you are indirectly boosting their ego for their ability to make a good decision, thus giving the caller a sense of importance. If you would prefer to think a little more outside the box and start with a more powerful presupposition, then you may want to consider something like "Thank you for calling (*your practice name)* my name is _____, and I am very excited to be talking to our next great success story . . ." This starter is very powerful and carries many strong assumptions. It starts by making the caller feel appreciated and important by beginning with a thank you, and is followed up with stating that you are excited to speak to them; another ego boost. Next, it indirectly suggests that your practice is very successful by using the phrase "our next great success story," which not only implies success, but great success. Finally, by answering the phone in this way, you have already embedded a suggestion for the caller's success. You can even replace the word "calling" to "choosing" to make it even stronger.

Now that you have a great starter, you need to complete the opener with a leading question or statement. You want to get your clients talking by asking something open ended that cannot be answered with a yes or no. Your goal is to get your clients to start talking about themselves and what they want to achieve right away. Here are a few examples of some leading statements that are effective at accomplishing this task: ". . . how can we help you succeed today?" ". . . what type of break-through can we help you to achieve?" ". . . please tell me all about the goals you are ready to accomplish?" ". . . what type of success do you seek today?" Open ended questions like these get the conversation started and most importantly, get the client to begin opening up immediately.

Here are few examples of effective ways to answer your phone:

"Thank you for calling (*your practice name)* my name is _____ and I very excited to be talking to our next great success story. What type of breakthrough can we help you achieve today?"

"Thank you for choosing (*your practice name)* my name is _____ . How can we help you succeed?"

"Thank you for calling (*your practice name)* my name is _____ . I'm very excited you called. Please tell me about the goals you are ready to accomplish?"

"Thank you for calling (*your practice name)* my name is _____ and I very excited to be talking to our next great success story. How can we assist you today?"

Compare the above examples to "The Hypnosis Center for Motivation and Habit Management," "Can I help you?" or "This is John Weir." These openers lead to nowhere, and the caller will feel disconnected from you. Plus, when phones are answered in this way, the next question is inevitably "How much are your services?" An ineffective salesperson answers this question, then the caller says thanks and hangs up the phone, and the sale is lost. Take a few minutes to create an opener that is similar to the examples above, and get the call on the right path from the very beginning.

Now that you have learned to answer the phone in a professional way, it's time to get your client to open up. Your goal is to get your clients to invest time into this phone conversation by asking them open ended questions related to their specific challenge. You achieve many things by getting your callers to talk about themselves.

First, it gives them the impression that you care about them because you are willing to listen.

Second, it enables you to build rapport by listening for ways to relate to them and uncovering their primary modality.

Third, you will discover all the key elements you need to hit on to sell this person on your services.

Finally, the more time a person invests, the more likely they are to work with you versus other hypnotists, even if they don't initially book with you. When a client calls the average hypnotist, they ask a question which the hypnotist answers, and no connection is ever really made. By listening to your client and giving them a mini phone consultation, you will make them feel valued and understood. You will create a connection with your client, and even if they don't book at the moment, they will come back to you because you listened to them. Plus, after a client has invested a good portion of time (10-20 minutes) discussing their problem, chances are low that they will want to go and explain that all over again to someone else. So, the majority of time they end up booking out of convenience.

While you are on the phone with a new client, never click off the line to answer your call waiting. Invest the time with your client and check your voice-mail after the call is over. The person on the phone could potentially bring in hundreds or thousands of dollars of business, so give them your full attention.

When the call first begins, steer clear of answering questions directly that could rapidly end the conversation. Initially, you want to avoid giving straight forward answers to questions like, "How much do your sessions cost?" "Do you offer group programs?" "How many sessions does it take to . . . ?" "Do you take insurance?" By directly answering these types of questions, you risk ending the phone call. Instead of directly answering these questions, you want to use an echoing strategy to elicit more information and get the client to continue talking. Echoing is a simple and effective strategy that can be done in several ways. The first and most powerful way to echo a client is by answering a question with a question. The second option is to quickly answer the question and rapidly respond back with another question. Finally, you can totally ignore their question and ask them something different.

Here are some examples of echoing:

Q: How much do your sessions cost?
R: Can you first tell me what you would like to accomplish?
(Echoing Strategy 1)

Q: How many sessions does it take to quit smoking?
R1: Can you tell me more about your habit?
R2: How much are you smoking now?
R3: Can you first tell me why you are ready to quit?

Q: Does insurance cover your services?
A: Yes, some insurance companies do cover hypnosis, but first I need to know what you want to achieve. Can you tell me more about your goals?
(Echoing Strategy 2)

Q: How many sessions does it take to help…?
R: Have you ever been hypnotized before?
(Echoing Strategy 3)

Always remember that the person who is asking the questions is the person who is in control. By echoing their question, you put the ball back in their court and you are able to immediately assume control of the conversation. This strategy helps to achieve two essential things. First, it will get the client talking, which gets them to invest time and energy into the conversation. This will help build rapport, and the more you get your client opening up, the more likely they are to choose you as their hypnotist. The second thing this strategy does is help to gather key information that can be used to sell your services. For instance, echoing can be used to elicit a person's buying strategy. Once you know this, you can virtually sell anybody anything. This can easily be done by echoing back a question like "what are you most looking for in a hypnotist?" or "what was it that made you choose the other hypnotist in the past?" (if they have worked with someone before). By echoing with a question like this, the client will inform you on all the things they are looking for.

They might answer, "the other hypnotist offered affordable sessions, a time that fit my schedule, and gave an audio program for reinforcement." When a client gives an answer similar to this, you know now exactly what needs to be done to sell this client. So a little later in the conversation when you are telling the client about your services, you will feed this information back to them with a line similar to this, "We have many great services we provide to our clients. First of all, we offer many different package deals to make sessions very affordable for our clients. We have a very flexible scheduling procedure, and we accommodate to our clients schedule and fit you in at a time that is most convenient for you. Finally, all of our private clients leave with an audio CD related to their challenge for ongoing reinforcement." When you feedback the clients buying strategy you elicited through echoing, it is very difficult for them to say no to you, especially since you are providing them with everything they were seeking. When the client is telling you how to sell them by revealing their buying strategy and you can't provide all of what the client is asking for, then match their strategy to the best of your ability. Depending upon the client and how big of a sale it is, you may consider working on developing the missing piece they are asking for just to land the client. For instance, if you were negotiating a deal with an office or corporation that liked when other trainers provided workbooks or training manuals to their employees, then you might want to develop one in order to book the client. If it's something that you could create before working with the client, then feed that back to them and start creating what your client would like to see done. .

Besides echoing, you will want to use open-ended questions to keep your clients talking and opening up. During this process it is suggested to jot down some notes about the client for future reference in the conversation, and for future sessions with them. Here are some examples of open ended questions hypnotists work with for common issues. Use questions like these to get the conversation going.

SMOKING CLIENTS:
Tell me about your habit. When do you smoke the most?
Why do you think you started smoking in the first place?
What have you done in the past to try and stop smoking?
Which groups of people do you smoke around the most?
Where are the places you smoke?
Why are you ready to quit now?

WEIGHT REDUCTION:
What do you need to improve to get healthier?
What type of emotions drive you to eat or snack?
What have you done in the past to reduce your weight?
Can you tell me about your weight goals?
Why are you motivated to change now?

STUDY HABITS/ TEST ANXIETY:
What areas do you need to improve in to improve your grades/ score better on tests?
In what ways have you experienced anxiety before an exam?

What distracts you in the classroom/ exam?

Can you tell me more about your current study habits?

Why do you want to improve your grades/ test scores?

What have you done in the past to prepare for a class/ test?

STRESS REDUCTION:

What are you currently doing to reduce your stress?

Can you tell me about what heightens your stress level?

Who/what creates the most stress in your life?

How is stress affecting your life?

What relaxation techniques have you used in the past?

FEARS:

Can you tell me when this fear started?

Can you tell me about how this fear is disrupting your life?

What is your typical response when confronted with your fear?

Do you believe this fear is rational or irrational, and why?

Have you ever tried anything in the past to overcome this fear?

What is motivating you to confront this fear now?

SPORTS PERFORMANCE:

What areas of your game do you want to improve?

What mental techniques have you used in the past that have worked?

Why did you decide to call our office?

Can you tell me a little about your current performance on the court/course/field/etc?

What upcoming goals do you have in your athletic career?

Can you tell me about the challenges you are currently experiencing?

SLEEP IMPROVEMENT:

Can you tell me about your sleeping habits?

Can you tell me about what goes through your mind when you are lying down?

How long has this been going on?

How is it currently affecting your life?

What have you done in the past to fall asleep?

What was going on in your life when this challenge started?

SELF-ESTEEM/ SOCIAL ANXIETY:

Can you tell me more about your personal/social challenges?

How do you know you are feeling insecure?

Can you tell me about your self-talk?

How would you like to live your life?

In what ways do you think hypnosis can help you?

What is motivating you to want to make a change?

What has stopped you from making change in the past?

By asking these types of questions, you accomplish many things. First of all, the client is focused on you and spending time talking to you, which increases the likelihood of a sale. Also, you get to gather valuable information about the client's challenge. This information can be used during your closing process when you book your session. This process is in a sense like doing an intake with a private client. During the intake, you elicit the information from them that is going to be used in the session. Like an intake, these initial phone questions will let you know exactly what the clients want, and more often than not, if you can provide your clients with exactly what they are after, you will close the sale. Keep in mind that some people will even feel obligated to say yes if you can give them what they want.

Now that you are getting your clients talking and opening up, the next thing you want to do during the phone call is classify the caller. All potential clients calling your office have many different levels of motivation and it's important to find out what type of caller you have on your hands. This is a key thing to do so that you will quickly be able to determine how hard you will have to work to close the sale. In my experience, I typically come across five different caller types.

These different types are listed below, followed by a brief description of each.

1. *THE READY AND WILLING:* This person has already made up their mind and they are ready to work with a hypnotist to achieve success. They are prepared to invest their time, energy, and money into a program. These clients more often than not know about the benefits of hypnosis and come from referrals, stage performances/lectures, or have used hypnosis in the past with great success. You can easily discern when this type of caller is on the phone, because they will commonly say things like, "my friend was just hypnotized and she is doing great," "I quit smoking through hypnosis many years ago and now I'm ready to address my weight problem," or "my doctor recommended your program and I want to book a session." These are clients you must close every time and schedule a session. If you can't seem to close these clients, then you must re-evaluate your closing strategies.

2. *ON THE FENCE:* This person has been contemplating making changes, yet has been procrastinating on making a full fledge decision to do it. These clients usually want to make a change, but just haven't found a way to achieve success. They may have had friends who have used hypnosis, but typically know very little about the process. If they did, they would probably be a "Ready and Willing" caller. "On the Fence" types usually have the money for a service, but since they typically don't understand hypnosis they are skeptical about moving forward. This type of caller needs to be convinced that they can be hypnotized and that they will be able to succeed with this process. These clients will reveal themselves by making statements like, "I really want to lose weight, but I know nothing about hypnosis," or "I was curious if hypnosis could help me with . . . ," or "My co-worker went to a hypnotist and it has seemed to help, but I'm not too sure about it working for me." Once you inform the potential client about the benefits of hypnosis and how easy it is to be hypnotized, you should be able to close these clients at a very high rate.

3. *THE BARGAIN HUNTER:* The bargain hunter is the person going through the yellow pages calling every hypnotist to find the cheapest price and/or best deal available. This caller has the perception that they can go to the cheapest hypnotist and still achieve the best success. The bargain hunter is very easy to identify. They will typically ask very direct questions and are very quick to the point such as, "how

much are your sessions?" "How many sessions does it take for…" or "Do your sessions have a guarantee?" These callers don't like to waste time because they are researching the field and want to call lots of places. The great thing about the bargain hunter is that they are sold on hypnosis, and they are usually ready to book a session if the deal is right. Money is usually the obstacle with these clients, and your job is to change the paradigm that cheap is better. We'll review how to do this in the coming chapters, but understand that if you can change this paradigm, it's very easy to book these callers. The other way to easily turn the bargain hunter into a client is to get them to invest time into the call. It is very important to get the bargain hunter to open up to you, and when you do it's simple to turn them into a client.

4. *THE MIDDLEMAN:* This caller is contacting your office for a loved one or a friend. These callers immediately reveal themselves with a statement like, "I'm calling for my husband" or "My mom asked me to call and get information." Your job with the middleman is to identify if they are the decision maker for booking the session, or if they are simply gathering information. If the middleman is the decision maker, then move in for the close in the typical fashion, but with a word of caution. When I have a middleman on the phone, a red flag immediately goes up in my mind, because often times these clients can be very difficult to work with. This occurs for a few reasons. First, the middleman is often times the one who wants the client to make a change, but the potential client really doesn't want to change. Also, hesitant clients typically have very low motivation, and if they were serious about making the change, they would have made the call themselves. There are some exceptions to the rule, such as the person being too busy to make the appointment, or the person having an unusual work schedule, like a graveyard shift. The final exception is that the person is physically unable to make the call due to illness or hospitalization. Always be sure to ask the middleman why the person was unable to make the call. If they don't fall into one of the appropriate exceptions, I suggest you have the middleman make the person call in themselves, or you run the risk of having a difficult or unmotivated client.

5. *THE CURIOUS GEORGE:* The Curious George is a caller who isn't very motivated to take action, but is just curious about hypnosis. The majority of the time, these callers read an article in the paper, saw something on TV, or came across something online. They are really only after information, and they reveal themselves by stating things like, "I just read an article about hypnosis and know nothing about it. Can you tell me more?" or "I saw this show on TV and wanted to know if hypnosis is for real." Also, they might say: "I read this article and wanted your opinion on this." These callers will make statements and ask questions that demand time and energy of yours, but they will not mention an interest in coming in for sessions. The Curious George has time on his or her hands, and is more than happy to waste your time if you are not careful. When talking with a Curious George, take control of the conversation by asking questions that require a personal response back, such as: "In what ways can my office help you?" or "How can we be of service today?" or "Are you ready to take action and book a session today?" Questions like these will help you to determine if the Curious George is worth speaking with on the phone. If they are not interested in taking action, refer them to your website or get

their address to mail out a brochure. Be sure not to waste too much time with an unmotivated Curious George. You can spend it in a more productive way by booking potential clients

Think about these different caller types when you receive incoming calls, so that you can begin to increase your success in selling your services. When you learn to identify the type of caller, answering the phone will become much easier as will booking new clients. You will soon become a master at persuading all types of people, and your schedule will be booked up for weeks.

The final concept I want to discuss in this chapter is what constitutes a successful phone call. In my opinion, there are only three things that signify success. The best indicator of success is getting a client's payment for their sessions on the initial phone call. When clients pay in advance, you know they are serious about creating improvements, and typically these clients will be great success stories. Plus, you already have the money in your bank account; a tangible sign of success. The second indicator of success is getting the client to commit and book a session with you. Nothing shows a successful closer more than a full appointment book. However, there is one other thing that is absolutely vital and must be done on every single phone call: remember to get the caller's e-mail address any way you can. This step is very important because not all clients are ready to move forward at the time of calling, and now you have a way to inform them of upcoming events and specials you are offering at your office. An e-mail list is the most inexpensive way to market your services. By gathering a caller's e-mail, you can stay at the top of his or her mind by sending e-mails which could possibly motivate them to take action in the future. E-mails also get forwarded around to families, friends, and office workers, so you never know who might find out about you simply by getting an e-mail address. Make getting an e-mail address a top priority, because they are worth their weight in gold. If all you do is collect an e-mail address and do not close the sale, the call is still a success.

As we continue on to more strategies for closing a sale, please keep in mind that the following strategies can be used both over the phone and in face-to-face selling situations. Incorporate these concepts into your phone calls for increased success and prosperity.

CHAPTER 6
SELLING VALUE

Now that you have gained rapport with your potential clients, whether it's face-to-face or over the phone, it's time to sell the value of your services. Once you get your client to open up, it's your chance to take over the conversation and begin the real persuasion process. Selling value is what it's all about, and when you successfully sell the value, the closing process becomes simple and seamless. In my professional opinion, selling value is the most important thing you need to learn in order to succeed in the profession. Learning to sell value will bring you more business than you can imagine, but failure to do it will be a surefire way to be out of business. This chapter is going to break down the importance of selling value, which areas you need to do this in, and how to do it by providing some examples of common challenges for hypnotists.

It's important to understand that people don't buy products or services; they buy the perceived value attached to it. Why do people spend $250 on a pair of designer jeans when they could buy a pair for $25? What drives a person to want to purchase a $75,000 luxury car compared to a $15,000 economy car that does the exact same thing? What motivates a person to work with a hypnotist charging $200 for a session instead of the person charging $50? Perceived value is the answer to all of these questions and that's what motivates people to take action on a service or purchase a product, not the product itself. Don't get me wrong, it is vital to deliver a good product or service, but in order to persuade people you must do more than just present a product or service, you must sell the value of it. People buy $250 designer jeans because that company has successfully attached tremendous value to owning their jeans. They attach feelings of popularity, success, trendiness, and importance to having their jeans. People are attracted to the idea that not everybody can have these jeans, so by having a pair it makes you stand out and show the world that you are a special and lucky person. People buy expensive cars or houses not to own something super expensive, but for power, status, feelings of importance, vanity, freedom, pride, happiness, and so on. Top salespeople sell the perceived value, not the product or service, because they understand it's these underlying factors that motivate people to take action.

One of the easiest strategies I have found to uncover the value of your services came from a master hypnotist and great friend of mine, Tom Nicoli. Tom told me that people are only interested in two things, and if you can answer these questions, you will get the sale the majority of the time. The two things people are most interested in are: "What's in it for me?" and "What's so great about that?"

Take a few moments and put yourself in the shoes of a potential client who is considering your services. Begin asking yourself the two questions stated above and write down the answers that come to you. If you were a smoker calling a hypnotist, ask yourself: "What's in this for me and what's so great about hypnosis?" The answers you come up with will more often than not be the underlying motivators that will truly get a person to take action.

The other important thing these questions will help you to achieve is to always think in terms of what the client wants and not what you want. For the majority of people, their favorite topic is themselves. The most commonly used words in the English language are I, me, my, and mine. It's important to keep this in mind while selling, because potential clients are not concerned with your needs or wants. They are only concerned with theirs. These questions help to train our minds to think only of the client's desires, and when you communicate in this way, you will notice an increase in your sales.

I'm sure you really want to uncover how hypnotists can get people to spend $200+ on a session while others can't get a client to book for $50. It's my opinion that there are two essential things you need to sell value on in order to achieve this. I believe you need to attach value to both your expertise and to your services in order to get your potential clients to say yes to your requests. Let's discuss these elements, and how to create value for these elements.

Hypnosis is a business where one is constantly aiming for more prestige. The more prestige you have, the more your services are valued, thus creating more sales at a higher rate. People want to go to the best, because this is the person they are confident can get the job done. When you work with hospitals, celebrities, or corporations, you build prestige and value into your name. You also create value through other third parties such as client testimonials, doctors and other referrals, as well as personal success stories. When talking with potential clients, if you can subtly weave some of these things into your conversation, it will help you establish yourself as an expert. However, please remember two things. First, never reference these third parties in an arrogant or boastful way. Weave them subtly and humbly into the conversation. Second, do not dominate the conversation with all of your accomplishments. Remember, most people are concerned with themselves, and want to be the topic of conversation. You just want to covertly plant the seeds that you are the person who can help them succeed. This can also be accomplished by referencing your website and informing them that they can go there to read client testimonials, and see a list of credentials.

The most important thing to create value around is the service you are providing. When you learn to sell the value and not just the service, it will make your job so simple. The ineffective salesperson only presents the product or service to the client with the hopes that it will sell itself. When a potential client calls and asks about an available program, the ineffective salesperson goes right into the details and outlines the program for the caller. For example they might say, "Our weight reduction program is 4 sessions, each session is $150 or $500 if you pay in advance. Would you like to schedule a session?" The typical response to a request like this will more often than not be a "no," because the salesperson failed to attach value to their services. You must understand that even if you are offering the best deal in the world, if you fail to attach value, then your sales will never reflect what your true potential. Effective salespeople have the magical ability to emotionally and mentally hook us to their product. They skillfully address their potential clients on an emotional level, and sell all the benefits that this product or service will bring into their clients' lives, rather than just presenting the product. These salespeople take time to think about what their client is really after, and they communicate in a way that brings up these emotions and connections. Remember, all that people care about are two things: "What's so great about this?" "What's in it for me?" The effective salesperson always answers these two questions for people, while at the same time attaching emotion, expectancy, and excitement to using a product or service. Let's now examine several examples of ways to attach value to hypnosis sessions. Use these examples as guidelines as you begin to think about how to attach massive value to your services.

SMOKE CESSATION CLIENTS:

1. "Now let me tell you about our smoke cessation program. Our program is designed to make becoming a non-smoker easy and effortless. This program has been instituted at many of the local hospitals to help their employees and patients put an end to this habit, and I know that you will be our next great success story. We help our clients eliminate their desire for cigarettes by removing resistance to the change, removing old associations to smoking, and linking up the old desire to drinking water. Our clients easily succeed without weight gain, and many experience the wonderful side effect of reducing their weight due to an increase in their water intake. The majority of people only need one session to successfully become a non-smoker, and our success rate is in range of 80% at a year follow up. Compare that to the 8-12% success rate of nicotine replacement therapy. The private session is two hours long, and during that time we will be discussing hypnosis so that you feel comfortable with the process, as well as discussing your habit more, and then doing the hypnotherapeutic session to get you on the road to success. You will leave feeling proud and confident that you will succeed for a lifetime. All clients also receive a home audio reinforcement program for ongoing success. I will be honest with you, though: most of my clients say they never listen to the audio, because they don't need it. Yet there are others that listen to it again and again because they love repeating the process. This program also comes with a lifetime service guarantee, which means that if you would ever go back to smoking, you can attend any one of our group sessions free of charge for life. The investment for the program is only $250. I have a session available this week on Thursday at 2:00 p.m. or on Friday at 11:00 a.m. Which works best for you?"

2. "I can completely relate to everything you are telling me, and let me tell you, I never anticipated how easy it would be to change once I was hypnotized. I smoked close to 2 packs a day, and after just one session, I have been a non-smoker for 8 years. It was so simple to change, and after I left I never had any real cravings. I just went about my business as a non-smoker, even while dating a girl who still smoked. It never bothered me. I am so excited for you because this one change brought so much success into my life and I know it will for you too. It feels so good to have more energy, more money, and the freedom is priceless. I want you to have the same success, and our program is a single session program that will put an end to this habit forever. The session is 2 hours long and we will spend our time together discussing the process, your habit, what needs to be done to succeed, and then you will experience the session. You will leave feeling confident about your success. I will also provide you with an audio reinforcement program for your home, and the program comes with a lifetime service guarantee. I am so confident in this program that if you would ever go back to smoking, you can attend any of our group

sessions free of charge for life. With a success rate that is over 80%, these groups tend to be very small, since most are enjoying their new lives as non-smokers. The investment for this program is only $250 and I know you are ready to book your session right away. Would you prefer a morning or afternoon appointment?"

3: "It really sounds like you are ready to succeed. Let me tell you about our program that has helped over 80% of our clients become non-smokers for over a year in just one session. Our program utilizes time-tested hypnotic techniques that will eliminate the desire for a cigarette. We know most people are concerned with gaining weight when they quit smoking, so that's why we link up that old desire to a new healthy habit like drinking water. Instead of reaching for a cigarette, our clients leave desiring water, which has post-hypnotic suggestions implanted to wash away all desire for a cigarette the moment you have a sip. We will help you dehypnotize your mind from all the false associations that were connected to a cigarette, such as the idea that you need to smoke when you drive, or that a cigarette provides pleasure. You will be able to overcome the resistance to the change, and simply go about your life as a happy, successful non-smoker. What will really impress you is how easy it is to make this change after our session is over, and you will leave feeling so proud of your decision to be smoke-free. This cutting edge program makes it easy to succeed. You will get a 2 hour private session, a home audio reinforcement program, and a lifetime service guarantee. Not to mention all the priceless benefits you receive as a non-smoker such as health, wealth, freedom, energy, pride, and so on. The investment is only $250 and I have two slots available this week. I have Tuesday at 3:00 p.m. or Friday at 10:00 a.m. Which works best for your schedule?"

WEIGHT REDUCTION EXAMPLE:

1: "Well, after listening to what you would like to accomplish, I want to let you know that I can definitely help you achieve success in these ways. Let me tell you about my program. My program focuses on helping people eliminate emotional attachments to food so that they can put an end to eating out of stress, boredom, reward, and so on. I will help you to train your mind to eat less but feel fuller and always satisfied. You will eliminate your resistance to exercise and link up positive feelings to moving your body more each day. Basically, I help you to take all the things you know you need to do and implement them into your life so you can take action. My clients typically reduce their weight 1-7 pounds per week and this program has been utilized in many of the local hospitals because of its effectiveness. The program is 4 weeks long with only one session per week, and the investment for the program is only $500, which is a savings of $100 off the private session rate. I have time available on Friday at 10:00 a.m. or 4:00 p.m. Which works best for your first session?"

2: "It sounds to me that you already know everything you need to be doing, and you have had success in the past reducing your weight. What makes our program so wonderful is that we can help you link positive feelings to living a healthy lifestyle so that you have a comfortable way of life rather than a struggle. Our program isn't a diet and doesn't focus on eliminating the enjoyment you get from eating. Instead, our program helps you to take back control of your eating habits, enables you to eat less and feel fuller, eliminate emotional attachments to food, and most importantly, change your perception about what types of foods are appealing to you. The program is 4 sessions, which meet once a week. During that time, you will boost your self-esteem as well as implement healthy habits that will produce results. You will be taught self-hypnosis for ongoing success and will be provided audio programs for reinforcement. The majority of clients reduce their weight 1-7 pounds per week and the success continues long after the program is finished. The investment is only $500 for the program and we can get you in this week or next week. How soon do you want to start your success?"

3: "Before going any further, let me congratulate you on this wise decision to become healthier and happier. This one decision to begin living a healthy lifestyle will bring so many wonderful benefits into your world. Most of our clients know what to do, but for whatever reason they are feeling stuck and having a hard time taking action. Our program eliminates the procrastination and resistance to living in a healthier way. We help you to easily move past those old blocks, while at the same time establishing healthy new habits that are simple and easy to implement. We help you to create a desire for healthy food, find enjoyment from exercising more, and boost your self-esteem. When you are finished with this program, you will have all the habits in place and know all the tools you will need to succeed for a lifetime. We focus on empowerment with our clients rather than dependency, so you will be taught self-hypnosis and will receive audio programs for ongoing success. The program itself is 4 sessions that meet once a week. During this month, new habits will be established and you will notice great success. Most clients reduce their weight 1-7pounds per week, and I know you will achieve similar if not better results. I know you are ready to get started, and you will be happy to know the investment is only $500 for the program. We have time available this week to get started. Would you prefer a morning or afternoon appointment for your first session?"

STRESS REDUCTION EXAMPLES:

1: "Well, it sounds to me like you really do need to develop some new coping strategies to deal with all these pressures in your world. Hypnosis is the easiest way not only to learn new stress reduction methods, but to implement new stress reduction strategies into your life. As a matter of fact, after the program is over, you will find yourself naturally responding to old stressors in a way you find to be most effective. Our program focuses on two things. The first focus is to help you eliminate daily stress. The process of hypnosis will naturally wipe the stress out of your life and have you leaving feeling calm, relaxed, and composed. We will also help you to develop new methods for reducing stress in a healthy way, rather than reaching for food, a drink, or a cigarette to help you cope. Plus, you will learn how to do self-hypnosis to help you succeed in all areas of life, and to reinforce your positive changes. This program has been used by hundreds of private clients as well as by employees of many local hospitals and companies. The program is 4 sessions long and meets once a week so that stressors can be identified and dealt with, and so that you can establish new stress reducing habits. You will even be provided an audio program for daily stress reduction and reinforcement. This program will help you take back control of your life and enable you to live in a healthier and happier way. The investment is only $500 for the 4 session program, and I can start you this week or next week. Which is best for you?"

2:    "It seems like this stress is causing a lot of problems for you, and I am confident that I can help you relax and learn better ways to let go of your stress. I'm sure you already know ways to let go of stress, but the challenge is getting yourself to use these techniques when you are truly feeling stressed out. That's where hypnosis comes in. What makes hypnosis so effective at helping people reduce and manage stress is that the message delivered in hypnosis can be accepted by both parts of the mind. This enables a person to take action on the new thoughts as a first and automatic response, rather than a resort back to unproductive or unhealthy responses like procrastination, smoking or snacking. Hypnosis enables you to easily implement these new techniques into your life and many other benefits will come with the process. You will lower your blood pressure, create more energy, feel happier, and handle life in a smoother way. So many people have benefited from learning to use their minds like this, and I am very excited you have decided to improve the quality of your life too. Our program is 4 sessions that meet once a week. During this time, we will change triggers to common stressors and install new stress management techniques that will work for you. You will be taught self-hypnosis for ongoing success and will be provided an audio program to repeat the experience at home anytime you wish. The investment is only $500 for the program, and you can do this in a private session or in a group session. Which would you prefer?"

I want to point out that these examples are not to be read word for word as a script. When selling the value of your services, you want to be sure that you come across smooth and natural. If you read the examples like a script, it will come across as rehearsed, and you risk losing the sale. You can certainly use the examples to sell your services, but just make sure that you get them down so well that it will come across to the client as something spontaneous and personal to them. However, your ultimate goal when selling the value of your services is to feedback some of the information you gathered earlier in the conversation. When you do this, you will reach your client on an emotional level that will greatly increase the likelihood of getting a yes to your requests. Use the above examples to generate ideas and as guidelines when you begin to move in for the close.

As you were reading the above examples, I am sure you were picking out some of the hypnotic techniques that were covertly woven into the beginning of the sales pitch. Think about selling a client as a waking hypnosis session, and use all the conversational hypnotic techniques you can think of in the persuasion process. When persuading my clients, I do whatever technique is necessary to get the client to say yes to my requests. I do this because I feel like I am doing them a service by persuading them, since I know they will benefit from my services and it will help them reach greater success in their lives. Here is one technique that is worth pointing out, so that you can utilize it when you are selling your services:

1. FUTURE PROJECTION/PACING: In one of the smoking examples, I used the line "The private session is two hours long, and during that time we will be discussing hypnosis so that you feel comfortable with the process and are able to discuss your habit more, and then we will do the hypnotherapeutic session to get you on the road to success. You will leave feeling proud and confident that you will succeed for a

lifetime." Using a pattern like this accomplishes several things. First, it projects the client into the situation, and forces the client to picture him or herself living out the described activity. Second and most importantly, it carries a heavy assumption that the client is coming to a session. For example, subtle statements like "we will be . . . ," and "you will leave . . . " strongly assumes that they have already said yes to coming in, and now you are just working out the details.

To sum up this chapter, let's do a quick review. After you get your client to open up and begin investing his or her time into your conversation, it's now time to assume control of the conversation and begin the persuasion process. The most important thing to do before moving in for a close or mentioning the price of your services is to attach value to your services. When you create value, you emotionally hook a client to what you are offering, especially if you feedback to them specific information gathered earlier in the conversation. You want to create value around your ability to get the job done by stating statistics, success rate, and/or third parties that you have worked with that raise your credibility. Then you will want to establish value in your services by informing the client of all the benefits and things they will receive by becoming a client of yours. Once you have created value, now it's time to let them know the price and move in for your first closing attempt. The closing technique used in the above examples was "The Either Or Assumptive Close," which will be explained in a later chapter. When you successfully establish rapport, get the client opening up, and sell the value of your service, then a simple close like the above examples is sometimes more than enough to get a person to say yes, especially if they are a ready and willing caller, or on the fence. Selling value is what it's about. Do this and watch your business grow. Fail to do this and watch your sales plummet. Take some time now to think about ways that you can build value around yourself and your services. Write down some answers and learn to skillfully weave these elements into the persuasion process.

CHAPTER 7
OVERCOMING OBJECTIONS

After you sell the value and go in for the first closing attempt, it is inevitable from time to time that you will come across objections to taking action on your requests. Please don't embrace false illusions by believing that everybody will jump at the chance to say yes to you. Expect a potential client to have objections, and learn to embrace the objections they have rather than retreating from them. Selling is nothing more than a grown-up game. The best salespeople in the world always experience objections during the persuasion process, but they have learned to play the game by overcoming the objections and closing the sale. Top producing salespeople welcome objections in the process because they know what to say to overcome the objection and close the sale. My father always told me that "objections are nothing more than buying signs." This observation has enabled my father to become very successful in the travel industry and it can help you in the profession of hypnotism. I was always told that as long as you are getting objections, you are still in the game. If people weren't interested, they wouldn't even bother bringing up their challenge. When people object to saying yes initially, it doesn't mean they are saying no to the service or product. What they are really saying is: "my conditions have not been met yet in order for me to say yes." When you are able to meet these conditions, or at the very least discover what they are and change the client's mind, then you will readily receive "yes" answers again and again. Overcoming objections and still getting the sale is such a fun game to play. When you begin to play the game, you will find that your ability to move past objections is easy and fun to do. You will find yourself getting so excited when your potential client has said no a number of times only to finally book their session at the end of the conversation. This chapter explains some easy to use strategies for overcoming objections. You will also be provided with a series of objections commonly heard by hypnotists, and several examples of how to handle them and assume control of the persuasion process. I know you are excited to learn to play the game of sales, so let's dive right in.

Before going on, I need to make an extremely important point clear to the new hypnotist/salesperson. When inexperienced people jump into the sales force, many people can become emotionally attached to their product or service, so that a potential client says no to their requests, it feels as if they are rejecting them personally. The inexperienced salesperson typically takes it personally, which causes them to feel as if they are no good or their service isn't worth what they are asking. Then, after hearing one too many no's, this salesperson is ready to find another job. Remember, they are saying no to the product or service, and not you.

My best and only sales training came from my work as a telemarketer. Telemarketing taught me some of the best lessons in sales I have ever learned. If you get a chance to spend a few weeks telemarketing, the experience is invaluable. Telemarketing taught me two very important lessons. The first lesson is that sales is a numbers game. It's wise to understand that NO leads to YES and I quickly realized in telemarketing that success greatly depended upon how many people I called. With every no I knew I was closer to a yes. The second and most valuable lesson telemarketing taught me was not to take rejection personally. I had to learn that the person wasn't saying no to me personally, but to the product I was offering. It wasn't personal because for whatever reason, it wasn't right for them at the time. So as you play the game of sales, understand that some people will say no to your requests from time to time. However, understand that it isn't because of you, but circumstances outside of you. You will notice though that when you begin master the skills outlined in this book, "no" will be a response you rarely hear. .

There are two very common ways to overcome objections that may arise from your requests. The first and easiest way to become proficient at plowing through objections is to be prepared. It would be advantageous to analyze your product or service and list as many potential objections to your service that you can think of. By analyzing the potential obstacles and jotting them on paper, you can now get to work on coming up with creative ways to move past these stumbling blocks. When you do your homework like this, you will be prepared for any and all objections, thus increasing your likelihood of carrying out a successful persuasion. This book helps you eliminate a lot of the leg work necessary for being prepared. Later in this chapter, you will read a series of objections that hypnotists commonly face and a variety of different responses you can use to overcome the objection. That way, you can begin moving in for the sale again. Just remember for now that preparation equals success.

Besides being prepared, you want to learn to overcome obstacles to the sale by learning to pace a person's objections. Just like pacing a person's behavior/ gestures to gain rapport, you can just as easily pace a person's objection to overcome it. Pacing a person's objection is executed by briefly agreeing with them, acknowledging (indirectly or directly) that their objection is valid, and then proceeding to sell them on a new idea. When you acknowledge that their objection is a valid point, this throws their mind off balance and makes them more receptive to the statement that follows. When most people offer up objections, they anticipate receiving resistance right back, or think that they can shut the salesperson down simply by posing an objection. However, by pacing the objection it interrupts their pattern, which in turn makes them more susceptible to suggestions (at least for a brief moment). This opens up a window to begin changing the paradigm that they uphold. Learning to pace a person's objections and change them into sales is truly a game. The more you enjoy playing the game, the easier it will be to move a person through the persuasion process.

The following examples were created to help you save some time preparing for future objections, as well as to provide you with some samples of how to pace an objection so that you can begin closing the client on your services.

OBJECTIONS TO THE NEW/YOUNG HYPNOTISTS
1. "You look really young." (We were wondering how old you were?)
Response A: "I know I'm young, and isn't it amazing that I found my passion in

life at such an early age?"

Response B: "I know I'm young, and isn't it exciting to see a person pursuing a professional dream?"

Response C: "I know. Sometimes I need someone to pinch me, because I am so young and already carrying out my purpose in life."

Response D: "Sure I'm young, but you don't have to be old to be great. There are many organizations with young professionals running the show, and doing a stand up job. For example, Pittsburgh's mayor is in his early 20s. Sydney Crosby is the face of a multi-billion dollar industry, and he is barely old enough to buy a beer. My youth is an asset because I bring fresh new ideas, enthusiasm, and professionalism to my work and I know I can be of service to you."

2. "How long have you been certified?"

Response A: "I received my certification a few months ago after completing a rigorous and intensive certification course. This course was all hands on, and I am very confident in my ability to be of service. I was also able to observe my instructor working with clients, plus I have been observed in real sessions by our instructor in order to demonstrate my competency and skills.

Response B: "I just recently received my certification, however, I have been studying hypnotism for a long time. I just finally decided to make it a profession."

Response C: "I received my certification a few weeks ago, and I am very excited to be taking on new clients. The people I have worked with so far have been great successes, and I know we are going to achieve great success together too. This is a great opportunity to schedule a session before things get too busy."

3. "You haven't been certified for too long. Do you think you could really help me?"

Response A: "It is true, I haven't been certified long, but I can definitely help you. I had extensive hands-on training in order to obtain my certification, and I had to consistently prove my competency to the instructor. I passed with flying colors and since starting my practice I have had great success."

Response B: "I know I haven't had my certification for very long, however I am very good at this work. Plus, since I am still new to the profession, you know I am going to be thoroughly prepared for our session, and you can count on me to deliver a powerful session for you."

4. "I have known you for a long time. Do you really think you could hypnotize me?"

Response A: "Just because we have been friends for a long time doesn't mean that you won't be able to be hypnotized. In fact, our friendship will work in our favor since you already feel comfortable with me."

Response B: "Yes, we have been friends for awhile, however it makes no difference if you have known me all your life or just met me for the first time. My job isn't to do something to you but rather serve as a guide in the process. What is important is that you have a willingness to follow directions and be hypnotized. Are you ready to be hypnotized?"

GENERAL OBJECTIONS

5. "I never knew that hypnosis costs so much money."

Response A: "I know at first glance that it may seem like a lot of money. When you really think about it though, you will come to find out that it is actually a very good investment in yourself. It is very difficult to put a price tag on things like an improved quality of life, more confidence, and a more optimistic outlook. These are priceless commodities, and the investment in my services is a small price to pay to learn how to use your mind more productively and see the results you desire. What other investment in the world can produce so many priceless returns on your investment?"

Response B: "I can completely understand if you didn't know how much hypnosis sessions were and if you are a little surprised with the price. However, since these services are effective and rapid, you end up saving a lot of money and time in the long run. You also escape the hassle of trying to figure out an answer to your problems. Plus, isn't time to invest in something worthwhile . . . like yourself?"

6. "That's a lot of money to pay in advance."

Response A: "You are right. It is an investment, but when you think it over, this investment will provide you with an amazing return. Plus, by making your investment in advance you save over $100! You do like saving money, right? We take all forms of payment except insurance. Which method would work best for you?"

Response B: "I know it seems like a lot of money, and after listening to you I really sense that you are ready to make this improvement in your life. You have suffered with this long enough, haven't you? And isn't it time to finally do something about it? I know you really want to come in for a program, and I want you to get the best deal. That's why it's best to pay in advance, so that you save over $100 and most importantly, finally get the success you deserve."

7. "Are your sessions guaranteed?" (Responses are only for people who are not offering a guarantee on their services.)

Response A: "I can completely understand why a person would want to seek a guarantee, especially with a process they know very little about. However, since this process greatly depends upon the client's participation, we cannot offer a guarantee on the session."

Response B: "Yes, we guarantee the session. We guarantee that you will be hypnotized, have a very enjoyable experience, and we will do everything in our power to help you succeed. Once you leave the office, it's your responsibility to carry out the suggestions, and since the success of the process is dependent on the client's participation, we do not offer a money back guarantee. When you are committed to achieving an outcome, a guarantee isn't necessary because you will succeed since you have made the decision to do so. I know what you're thinking: you are one of the committed ones, and I know you can achieve this goal with a little help. You know it's time to make this happen and you deserve to have this success in your life."

Response C: "It's true that some products come with a guarantee, but in this profession we aren't dealing with a product that you can return, we are working with unpredictable human behavior. It's impossible to predict the actions of other people, and would be impossible to do it in this case. In the same way, doctors and psychiatrists can't guarantee their work, since much of the success is the responsibility of their client, which is out of their control. Plus, since you are committed to change, there would be no need for a guarantee. We want you to come into the office with an attitude expectant of success, and we can help you achieve just that."

8. "I tried hypnosis before and it didn't work." Why should I try it again?

Response A: "I have worked with many people that have tried hypnosis unsuccessfully in the past, only to help them finally succeed with the process. Sometimes, it's the hypnotist's fault for not clearly informing you of what to expect during your session. With all new clients, we take the time to properly educate you on hypnosis so that everyone knows what to expect, and how to notice the changes in their life."

Response B: "In all professions, there are great, mediocre, and bad professionals. If you went to a doctor that wasn't good, you would find a new doctor, not dismiss the field of medicine for not being effective. The same is true about hypnosis. It is true that there are some hypnotists out there who are less effective than others. It's not a matter of if hypnosis will work or not, but more a matter of finding the right hypnotist for you. Our center has a good track record of success, and I know we can help you finally achieve the success you have always wanted."

Response C: "Everybody experiences the world differently, and it's up to the hypnotist to determine the best induction method for their client. If the induction method wasn't matched up right, it can be difficult to create success. All of our hypnotists know a variety of different techniques to induce hypnosis, so there is no question that you will find the right method for you. We also take the time to do an assessment to ensure that you are getting the best induction and suggestions that are tailored to your needs, not just a generic script."

Echoing Response: "It didn't work? (Sometimes using an echoing strategy in a position like this is the best response. The statement, "I tried hypnosis and it didn't work" is so vague that it could mean anything. This statement could mean that they weren't able to be hypnotized, that it didn't work long term, it didn't work to their satisfaction, it didn't work at all, or any number of other things. By echoing a question back to them, it forces them to answer the question more specifically, and will provide you the information you need to successfully overcome the objection).

9. "I need to talk it over with my husband/wife."

Response A: "I can understand your desire to talk it over with your significant other, but please understand that this is your decision, not theirs. You will be the one who has to invest the time and energy into accomplishing your goal, and ultimately it is your decision whether or not to pursue this goal of yours. Isn't now the time to make the decision to improve the quality of your life?"

Response B: "I can understand your desire to talk things over with your significant other, however, I know that you know if this is something that is going to make you happier and healthier, they would be all for it. It sounds to me like you are ready to make this change, and the only challenge is that I fill sessions very quickly. If it takes a long time to sit down and talk it over, it might be a few weeks until I can get you into the schedule. Why don't we pencil you in now, and then you can talk it over with your husband/wife. That way, you have your space saved, you won't have to wait a few weeks for your first session, and you can still get their blessing on you creating this success in your life."

10. "That session time doesn't fit into my schedule."

Response A: "I completely empathize with your situation, and not having enough time in the day, yet we do make exceptions in our busy schedule all the time for things that are really important, like visits to the doctor. You know this is something that is important to you and definitely deserving of your time. If you are worried about your boss giving you some time to come to our appointment, I would be glad to write you a note to give to him or her."

Response B: "I know life is hectic, and most people are very busy; that is even more of a reason to come in. Many people get so caught up in the crazy pace of the world that they forget to take time to unwind. I know you make exceptions for visits to the doctor, so why not make an exception for yourself right now."

11. "Do I really have to go to all of those sessions?"

Response A: "It is a commitment to make it to every session, and yet like any process, you need to complete the entire program. The number of sessions is designed for your success, because for long term behavioral changes to take place you need reinforcement and encouragement of the new behavior. You do want to be a long term success, don't you?"

Response B: "I know it sounds like a commitment, and in a way, it is. Sometimes, due to Hollywood's portrayal of hypnotism, people sometimes think of hypnosis as a magical formula that will instantly correct all behaviors. In reality, hypnosis is like all other therapeutic vehicles in the fact that it requires reinforcement and encouragement to ensure long term behavioral change. The great thing is, this process is very efficient compared to other traditional modalities."

12. "I have to think it over."

Response A: "I know this is a lot of information to sort out, however, something prompted you to call today. Is it really worth spending any more energy on this old problem? I know you know it's time to make this change, so why don't we at least take the first step towards success today by penciling you into a time slot. Then you will have a few days to think it over, and if you change your mind you just give me a call. I am positive that once you take that first step, you will absolutely know it's the right time for you to succeed."

Response B: "I know it can be tough making a decision when there are so many options to achieve this goal. I know you want to think it over, but would you be so kind as to tell me what is the only thing that is preventing you from now taking action?" (This powerful question will help to elicit the real objection they are trying to work out. More on this later.)

13. "I talked to another hypnotist and they were cheaper."

Response A: "It is true that there are some hypnotists that are cheaper in the area. However, let me give you a valuable piece of advice. Whatever you do, don't select a hypnotist based on price. It's best if you select the one who has a proven track record of success, and someone you have rapport with. Even if it's not me, please make a promise to yourself to make the selection based on qualifications and rapport, not price. Because in the long run you will end up going to the more expensive hypnotist anyways, once you get what you pay for with the other one."

Response B: "I understand that but let me ask you a question. If you or a loved one needed to get heart surgery would you bargain shop for the cheapest heart surgeon? If you needed to rewire your house would you look for the cheapest electrician to do the job? Of course not. You would go to the person you could rely on and trust to get the job done right. Don't make your decision based on price ... make your decision on the person who can get the job done right. That's an intelligent decision, isn't it? I have a session available on Tuesday or Thursday. Which would you prefer?

14. "Will you match someone else's price?"

Response A: "Shopping around for a good price is an excellent strategy in many buying situations, but when looking for someone to help you succeed, your decision should be based more on their ability to get the job done rather than the cost. Our service is unique to all others, and because we offer a program different than the rest, we do not match other hypnotist's prices. However, since you are seeking the best price to achieve this goal, let me tell you about our package deals that can save you a lot of money."

Response B: "Since no two hypnotists are alike, it is very hard to match another person's price. When you invest in us, you can be confident that you are investing your time with experienced professionals that have a proven track record of success. I am confident we can get the job done and by getting it done right the first time, we will save you a lot of money in the long haul."

15. "I don't know if hypnotism would work on me."

Response A: "Everybody can be hypnotized, since all you have to have is a desire to improve your life. All it takes is following simple step by step instructions. These instructions are so simple that my little cousins who are 7 and 8 years old can easily follow them".

Response B: "Everybody can be hypnotized because everyone is suggestible. If you weren't suggestible, you couldn't learn. Being hypnotized is just learning to use your mind in a more productive way, which speeds up the change process. You do want to succeed sooner than later, right? Well, hypnosis can help you succeed with lightning speed. Knowing this, are you ready to take action now?

Response C: "In a nutshell, our mind's primary job is to act out our dominant thoughts and statements. Look at how well you have been hypnotizing yourself and how your mind has been acting out the very thing you don't want. Isn't now the time to finally give yourself some new thoughts to act out? Maybe ones that are more important to you?"

Echoing Response: "Won't work for you?" (Use a question in these situations to get a more specific answer from your client rather, than assume it's something it's not.)

Take time to create your own responses to some of these common objections. Come up with creative ways to pace your client's objections and flip them into selling opportunities. Welcome all objections, because once you know the hurdle, you can figure out a way to clear it.

CHAPTER 8
CLOSING STRATEGIES

Now that you understand how to move past objections, it is essential that you begin to develop some closing strategies to move the persuasion process along. The strategies outlined in this chapter are proven effective when selling hypnosis, and can be used at any point of time after selling the value of your services. This chapter will cover a variety of different ways to close clients on your services, and these strategies can be implemented in face to face selling as well as selling over the phone. The strategies outlined here will provide you with the remaining tools necessary to become a master persuader.

Let's start this chapter off with a technique called the "Scale of Readiness." After your potential clients have told you about their problem, you can follow up this information with a simple yet powerful question that is designed to elicit their readiness to take action. The question is simply "on a scale from 1-10, 10 being the most motivated, where are you in your readiness to correct this problem and now take action?"

This question is powerful for several reasons. First, when a person tells you their readiness to make the improvement, they are indirectly telling you how ready they are to be closed on your services. This will key you in right away on how hard you will have to work to close the client. The potential client's response will also help you to classify your caller, as outlined in Chapter 5. Obviously, if you have a client tell you they are at an 8, 9, or 10 on the scale, it's going to be easier to sell them and you should move right in for the close. However, when the client is in the middle of the scale, you will know right away that this client will require a little more effort in the closing process. Very rarely do I come across clients on the low end (5 or less) of the scale. When the client is on the low end of the scale, it is important to still attempt a persuasion. If you find the client doesn't become more open, you are better off giving them some literature or referring them to your website rather than wasting more of your time. Some people just aren't ready, so put your focus on more important tasks.

The second reason this question is effective is because of the embedded command at the end. You may have been wondering why the words "now take action" are italicized, and this is to indicate a shift in tonality. As you ask your clients this question, slightly change your tonality and slow down your speed when saying the words "now take action." When you do this, it will embed the suggestion into the subconscious mind due to the subtle shift in tone and speed. Later on, when you are requesting them to take action, the mind will remember your suggestion, and greatly increase the chances of a successful close.

Finally, this question can help to uncover the client's real reason for wanting to make the change. Sometimes the clients will spontaneously provide their true motives for change, or the main reason for not taking action. If they don't, you can follow up the scale of readiness question with another powerful question that will pull this information out of them. The question is "what is the only thing holding you back from making this change now?" This question is useful for eliciting valuable information that can be leveraged later in the persuasion process to move them along. It also is very assumptive in the fact that there is only one thing stopping them from saying yes to your requests. By subtly emphasizing only, it is a strong suggestion to the client's mind to find only one thing that is preventing them, rather than a laundry list of objections. Also, by embedding the words 'change now,' you are covertly suggesting to the subconscious to change, whether that be changing their thoughts about saying yes to booking a session or yes to making the change they desire now. Either way, this embedded command is very strong in helping you close the sale. Once the client answers this question, you have now determined exactly what needs to be done to close them. The beauty of this simple technique is that the client will give you every bit of information necessary to get their business. Then all you have to do is gracefully echo back this information to them, and you have yourself a new client.

Another strategy that you can use in persuasion is the process of creating YES SETS. A Yes Set is a powerful process that puts your client in an agreeable mindset as you move in for the close. The way to execute the Yes Set process is by asking a series of questions that are said in a specific way to elicit only a "yes" response. Once you have momentum on your side and the client has answered yes several times in a row, you follow it up with a leading statement or a close. Utilizing this process in the selling process and in your hypnosis sessions will dramatically increase the likelihood of a successful persuasion.

Your goal with any persuasion is to bypass the critical factor so that your client will non-critically accept what you are offering; the same as it is in hypnosis. It's important to understand that every agreement, whether out loud or internally, subtly lowers the critical factor because the conscious mind believes that you are someone they can trust because you are telling the truth. When this occurs, the critical factor relaxes, and the client's mind becomes more suggestible and receptive to requests. So, how is this done?

In order to create a Yes Set, you must first take some time to think about several undeniable truths that can be used in the persuasion process. An undeniable truth is something that the client can't disagree with or say "no" to. An undeniable truth could be as simple as, "It's a beautiful day isn't?" "You were calling because you want to succeed, right?" or "Smoking will eventually cause damage to the body." You can deliver undeniable truths as questions or as statements. It is my belief that in the selling process it is more powerful to use questions, because questions force the client to be active in the process of agreeing, thus making their mind more agreeable to later suggestions. However, when you deliver a question to elicit only a "yes" answer, it must be done in a specific way. The way to deliver the questions is in the form of AFFIRMATIVE INFLECTION STATEMENTS or A.I.'s. A.I. statements are questions which are delivered as a statement. In other words, these questions are said with a downward inflection at the end rather than an upward one. By delivering the questions with a downward inflection, you are not really asking a question, but saying it in a way that is just seeking agreement from the person. If you were to write out these questions, you would end the question with a period, not a question mark. There are several different types of A.I. statements that can be used.

The first type is a regular A.I. statement. These statements have the tag question at the end of the sentence. Here are several examples:

"It's a beautiful day, isn't it."

"That sure felt great, didn't it."

"That's a comfortable chair, huh."

"You have driven your chair on autopilot before, haven't you."

The second type is the backward A.I. statement. With the backward A.I. statement, you put the tag question at the beginning of the statement.

Here are some examples:

"Isn't it a beautiful day."

"Didn't that feel great."

"Isn't that the most comfortable chair."

"Wasn't that experience wonderful."

The third type is called the feedback A.I. statement. These statements use tag questions to affirm what the client has said. When the client is right, add a tag question as a response back, and it makes them affirm what they said all over again. Here are some examples:

Client: "It's a beautiful day outside."

Response: "Isn't it."

Client: "That felt amazing."

Response: "Didn't it."

Client: "That is a great deal."

Response: "Isn't it."

The final type is a non-verbal A.I. statement. This is simply a head nod "yes" or even sometimes "no". When you see a person nodding their head up and down, you instinctively think "yes" in your mind. During face to face sales, you can use a head nod to affirm, and subconsciously get the client's mind thinking "yes" as they are talking about taking action. You can also combine the head nod with the other A.I. statements to add even more influence, and to further confirm agreement from your client.

After a series of undeniable truths or A.I.'s, you now have the client in an agreeable mindset. Now it is time to deliver your suggestion, which may or may not be an undeniable truth. In the selling process, this would typically be a closing line, or any other suggestions that request the client's commitment to your services. By delivering your requests in this fashion, you dramatically increase the likelihood of success, because you have the client already in a habit of saying "yes" to you.

The pattern that I use when I am persuading potential clients, writing business letters, or developing hypnotic scripts is as follows:

1. Truth, truth, truth, persuasion
2. Truth, truth, persuasion, persuasion

3. Truth, persuasion, persuasion, persuasion
4. Persuasion until conclusion

The first set of examples demonstrates how to use simple A.I. statements to get the client in an agreeable mode. The second series will include more complex examples of how to use this formula to sell your services. Let's examine this process in action.

SIMPLE EXAMPLES OF A.I.'S:
1. "Hypnosis is a fascinating subject, isn't it?" (truth) "Watching a stage performance does make it easy to wonder what the potential of the human mind really is, doesn't? it" (truth) "I'm sure you would agree that we haven't even discovered our full potential yet, huh?" (truth) "Wouldn't it be amazing to come in for a session and experience it now for yourself?" (persuasion)
2. "I'm sure you have read articles talking about the success of hypnosis, haven't you?" (truth) "Isn't it amazing how powerful the mind is?" (truth) "Don't you find those success stories fascinating?" (truth) "I know you are ready to achieve success like that, aren't you?" (persuasion)
3. "I understand that you know nothing about hypnosis, right?" (truth) "I'm sure when you think about hypnosis you probably think about stage performers or the Hollywood image, huh?" (truth) "When you see something like this, it provokes a lot of questions in one's mind, doesn't it?" (truth) "If I was able to inform you of the truth about hypnosis, you would be interested in finding out more, wouldn't you?" (persuasion)

I'm sure you get the idea of how to use simple A.I. statements to get the mind in an agreeable state. Have fun with A.I. statements and use them to your advantage to get more positive responses. Now let's look at a few more examples that are slightly more complex. These examples incorporate undeniable truths in a different fashion than the above examples, yet they achieve the same results. Remember, when an undeniable truth is presented to the mind, the mind becomes more receptive and open.

SMOKING CESSATION EXAMPLE:
1. "You know that this habit is costing you lots of money (truth 1), you told me it was hurting your health (truth 2), and it's becoming a big inconvenience for you (truth 3). I know you are now realizing that it's time to do something about this (persuasion). Hypnosis is clinically proven to be a very effective way to become a non-smoker (truth 1). I know most people are concerned with the typical withdrawals (truth 2), but did you know that most people are able to become a non-smoker in a session or two with hypnosis (persuasion and embedded command for success)? Isn't now the time to make an investment in yourself and get the success you deserve (persuasion)? I see clients Monday through Friday, and my last session is at 6 pm (truth 1). Would you prefer your session in the morning or afternoon (persuasion and close)? I have a session on Tuesday at 3:00 p.m. or Friday at 2:00 p.m. Which would prefer (persuasion and final close)?"

WEIGHT REDUCTION EXAMPLES:
1. "I bet you are like most of my clients and have tried all the diets (truth 1), only

to lose the weight (truth 2) and put it right back on again (truth 3), but hypnosis is a more effective method because it helps you create a healthy lifestyle (persuasion). A healthy lifestyle not only helps a person reduce their weight, (truth 1) but it enables a person to maintain their success (truth 2). You do deserve to have long term success, don't you (persuasion)? Hypnosis is just the way to do it in an easy yet effective way (persuasion). I know you would like to be like my clients and reduce your weight 1-7 pounds per week, (truth) and now is the time to take action (persuasion) because you deserve to finally get the body you have always wanted (persuasion). We offer both private and group sessions. How would you like to succeed (persuasion + close + embedded command)? There is a group session that starts on the 25th or one a few weeks later on the 7th. Which one would you like to join (persuasion and final close)?"

2. "Statistics say that 98% of all diets fail (truth 1), and the reason they fail is because they are focused on short term changes rather than lifestyle changes (truth 2). They also fail to correct a very important issue (truth 3), and that is a person's emotional attachments to food (persuasion). I bet you are like most of my clients, and eat for reasons other than hunger, right (truth)? Many people find themselves eating out of boredom, stress, loneliness, and reasons other than hunger (truth). One of the reasons hypnosis is so effective is because it helps you to put an end to emotional attachments to food so that you can finally be back in control of your eating habits (persuasion). Wouldn't it be incredible to be totally in control of your health and to find it easy to make the right choices (persuasion)? By removing emotional attachments to food, you can create significant weight reduction because you will have eliminated so many mindless, unnecessary calories (truth). I can help you to reach your goals (persuasion), and you will find hypnosis to be the most effective method you have ever experienced (persuasion). I know you are excited to get started, and I can get you into my office either on Wednesday at 11 a.m. or at 6:00 p.m. Which would you prefer (persuasion + close)?"

CORPORATE STRESS REDUCTION EXAMPLE:

1. "I know that you are well aware that stress decreases productivity (truth 1), increases employee sick days (truth 2), and increases harmful habits like smoking, drinking, and overeating (truth 3). Our Corporate Stress Reduction program will help your employees effectively deal with the stresses of life which will increase company productivity (persuasion). The same way stress increases negative habits like smoking (truth 1), it also drives up insurance costs due to all the increased sick days caused by stress and these negative habits (truth 2). Your company could use a stress reduction program for your employees (persuasion) because don't you enjoy when your company saves money and is very productive (persuasion)? Everybody is feeling the burden of these tough financial times (truth), your employees would benefit tremendously from learning these techniques (persuasion), and it's an investment that everybody profits from (persuasion). By now I'm sure you are thinking this is something your company could definitely use and so the only question that remains is how soon you want to help your company succeed with this program(persuasion + embedded commands + close).

After reading through these examples, you have probably become aware of the simple closing line that is attached to the end of each example. This is a perfect time to introduce you to one of the simplest yet most effective closing strategies in existence and that is the EITHER OR ASSUMPTIVE CLOSE. The Either Or Assumptive Close is what I use the majority of the time when I am closing the deal with my clients. Master this simple strategy and watch your sales skyrocket!

Let's start by looking at a few examples of this closing strategy, and then I will breakdown why it is so effective in the persuasion process.

A: "I have time available on Thursday at 2:00 p.m. or Friday at 11:00 a.m. Which works best for you?"

B: "Do you prefer to have your session in the morning or afternoon?"

C: "We offer both private sessions and group programs. Which type of session would most suit your needs?"

D: "Our private clients book sessions in blocks of 3, 5, or 8. Which package is best for you?"

E: "You can either book a private session now or get a download that you can use from your home. How would you like to create this improvement in your life?"

These are all examples of the extremely effective *EITHER OR ASSUMPTIVE CLOSE*. This simple strategy is very powerful for several reasons. The first reason is that it's strongly assumptive. It's worth mentioning that master salespeople possess a very assumptive attitude when it comes to selling their product or service. They assume the clients want what they are offering and maintain that attitude throughout the persuasion process. This particular closing strategy strongly assumes the sale, and the real question isn't if the client wants your service, but more a question of how and when. By asking the client, "I have a session this week on Thursday at 2:00 p.m. or 6:00 p.m. Which is best for you?" You assume they are coming in. You also change the client's focus from if it's right for them to what time is the best for them. When they answer the question, they have indirectly said "yes" to your requests and you have closed the sale. Now all you have to do is gather their information, inform them of any instructions you have for them before their session, and end the call.

It is appropriate now to bring up the golden rule of sales, and that is to learn to *shut up*. One thing that is absolutely vital to the success of this closing strategy is when you ask a question such as "I have a session this week on Thursday at 2:00 p.m. or 6:00 p.m. Which is best for you?" you must do whatever it takes to shut up, be quiet, and not say another word. It is possible to talk yourself out of sales and this is the time in the process it can occur. It's very important to know that at this point in the game, the person who talks first loses. If you use the Either Or Assumptive Close and talk before your client answers, you have lost the sale. However, if you wait it out, chances are you will book the session. Take my word for it, I have talked myself out of many sales early on in my career, and by learning to be quiet I greatly increased my closing rate. Again, once they answer, go right into information gathering and then end the conversation.

The second reason this closing strategy is so effective is that it provides the client a false sense of choice or control in the situation. People like to be in control, especially when it comes to making a decision that involves a purchase. This method provides the client with a choice to make, but the options are something that favors you either way. For example, imagine you wanted to go to the movies, and you wanted to see an action film or a comedy rather than the other types available. It is more effective to ask, "Let's make tonight movie night. Would you rather watch a comedy tonight or would you prefer an action film?" Instead of asking, "What movie would you like to see?" The first question assumes that they want to go to the movie without directly asking them, as well as gives them the option of picking the type of movie to watch. The beauty is that both of the available choices are what you want. This lets you benefit by seeing what you want to watch, as well as makes the other person happy because they feel like they made the selection. If you ask the question the second way, you leave the door open to a number of possibilities that you may or may not want as well as leaves the worst possible answer in the game, which in this example would be, "I don't want to watch a movie." When using this technique, make sure that the options you provide help to achieve the outcome you desire, as well as what the client desires. For example, "I know you are ready to succeed with hypnosis, and the only question left is if you want to do the program in a private session or would you prefer to get an audio program to use in your home?" Either way the client answers, you have created a sale.

This close works for me virtually every time and I strongly suggest mastering this simple strategy. On the rare occasions when a client answers, "I might have to think this over and call you back" or "I'm not sure yet," here are a few follow-up responses that will help to identify the actual objection and flip it back into a closing attempt.

Response A: "What is the only thing that is preventing you from now taking action?"

This is an effective way of responding back, because it also carries a strong assumption and an embedded command to assist in the persuasion process. The presupposition in this question is "what is the only thing." The word only makes the strong assumption that there is only one thing holding them back from making the decision right now. When they answer the question, they confirm in their subconscious mind this assumption, and once you know what you need to overcome, you can easily proceed to closing the sale again.

The second half of this question is an embedded command to get the person to take action and book a session. Remember, when you are talking over the phone, more is said by how you say something rather than the words. By slowing down your delivery slightly, the subconscious mind hears it and says to itself "this is important." This embedded command is going to be activated as soon as you overcome the objection they tell you. People like to be known as an action taker and it's important that once you create a solution to their challenge, you move back in for the close. For example, if it's a money issue and the client can't afford your private sessions, you can solve their problem by signing them up for a more affordable group session or sell them your audio programs. Once you solve their problem, close them again. Here are a few other examples of good responses:

Response B: "If I was able to save you some money are you willing to take action now?"

Response C: "If I was able to provide you with a free audio program are you ready to take action now?"

Response D: "If I was able to throw in an additional session at no charge are you ready to take action now?"

Response E: "If I was able to throw in a gift certificate for a group session are you ready to take action now?"

Using these types of responses lets you assume control of the situation again and also pushes the client to make another decision. However, this time there is an additional incentive to say "yes". With this added incentive, you make the client feel like they are getting a better deal and you then increase the likelihood of closing the sale. This response also contains an embedded command to encourage the client's subconscious mind to go along with the persuasion process.

Now let's examine the *Buy Now* closing strategy. This strategy is very effective, and can be utilized as your first closer or immediately following a response to an objection to your services. Let's go over several examples of this simple closing technique, and then we will breakdown why it's effective.

Example 1: "By now, you know everything you need to know about hypnosis and our programs. The only question that's left is how soon you will be enjoying the benefits of creating success in your life?"

Example 2: "By now, you have learned how hypnosis helps people quit smoking, all about our program, and our guarantee. The only question that now remains is how soon you will be enjoying all the benefits of being a non-smoker?"

Example 3: "By now, you know that establishing a healthy lifestyle is the way to achieve permanent weight reduction and you understand how hypnosis makes this a reality. The only question that now remains is how soon you want this success in your life?"

Example 4: "By now, it's easy to understand how hypnosis can help you succeed in this area. You have answers to all of your questions and know all about our services that will help you succeed. The only question that needs to be answered is how quickly do you want this success in your life?"

Example 5: "By now, you have told me how this challenge is holding you back and giving you less than you deserve. You have been informed about how we can assist you in a rapid way, and you now know that you have the ability to be hypnotized. The only question that is left is how soon do you want to make this improvement?"

The *Buy Now* strategy is effective for several reasons. First, the words *Buy Now* are linguistically ambiguous, which means they carry two meanings. The words can be interpreted as by now (a moment in time) or as buy now (a direct request to buy). When you deliver the words by now as an embedded command, the subconscious picks it up as an action request, not a moment in time. It is important to subtly change your tone (i.e. lower your voice) and pause slightly after saying the words "by now." This will make the phrase stand out to the subconscious mind and go in as an indirect suggestion. Target Department Stores used this strategy in one of their ad campaigns. They used the song "Hello, Good Bye," but on the screen they printed the words "Hello, Good Buy," and then flashed their new products. Even though this method was very obvious, it definitely makes an impression on the subconscious mind. The next time the consumer is shopping at

Target and he or she sees something they like, the subconscious says "Hello Good Buy." I thought this was a brilliant ad campaign and it was encouraging to see a big corporation using this simple yet very effective strategy.

This strategy also incorporates pacing and leading. In the above examples, the embedded command to "*BUY NOW*" is immediately followed up with a pacing statement or an undeniable truth. This is done in order to get the mind in agreement again, especially if the phrase is used after overcoming an objection. By pacing the potential client and saying something they can't deny, you lower the critical factor momentarily, thus making the client more receptive to your next closing attempt.

The third element of this strategy is the closing question. This question is a strong presupposition that assumes that all of the client's questions and objections have been resolved, which means all that's left is to make a final decision. The closing question also strongly assumes that they have agreed to your requests by using the phrase "how soon you will be enjoying the . . ." This statement covertly suggests to the mind that the client will be enjoying the benefits, and now the question is how soon rather than if.

Finally, this strategy finishes with yet another embedded command to take action or anchor the positive benefit of your services to the request. Insert an embedded command that is relevant to your client in the underlined sections of the given examples.

The final closing strategy that will be discussed is called the *PRO AND CON CLOSE*. The *PRO AND CON CLOSE* is very straightforward, and can be very effective, especially in face to face selling situations. In this closing strategy, your job is to get the client to create a list of the pros and cons for taking this particular action in their life. Your job as the salesperson is to get the clients to physically write out both the benefits of taking action, and the cons of staying in their present position. Getting your clients to write it out will aid the process in a couple of ways.

First, writing out the pros and cons forces the client's mind to critically think about the situation. The client's critical factor will always work in your favor in this situation, especially because it's the part that has been pinpointing their behavior enough for them to decide to make the call. Second, writing out thoughts makes an impression on the subconscious mind. This occurs because the process takes something intangible (a thought) and makes it tangible (message on paper). That is why this process is always suggested when formulating goals. Writing it out is as effective in the selling process as it is in goal setting. Finally, it provides a non-verbal and visual close to the client. It is very difficult to say "no" to something when you are aware of all the benefits compared to one or two cons. This strategy is very easy to understand, and listed below are two examples of how to apply this strategy in the persuasion process.

SMOKING CESSATION EXAMPLE:

Pros: improved health, more money, better quality of life, set a good example, look younger, have more energy, be there for the grand kids, earn respect at work, have more control . . . etc.

Cons: $250 for the smoking program.

Closing Question A: "Aren't your health, respect, and grandkids worth a $250 investment? And, as long as you are committed to success, this is an investment that will pay itself back many times over." *INSERT CLOSING STRATEGY OF CHOICE.*

WEIGHT REDUCTION EXAMPLE:

Pros: Look better, greater confidence to attract a significant other, more attention, more energy, more active, and social lifestyle, greater control . . . etc.

Cons: Commitment of time and money.

Closing Question A: "I know you are an intelligent person, and as you look at that list what do you think is the best decision to make?"

Closing Question B: "Aren't your body and your life worth a small commitment of your time each week?"

I know at first glance that this strategy may seem too simple to work, but it does. Never underestimate the power of the Pro and Con close. This technique will work over the phone, and it is even more effective in person. You can use this as a starting strategy to elicit valuable information, and move in for the close. It is also effective as a last resort to help seal the deal or to identify any last objections that may surface during the selling process.

Sales is a game, and when you utilize these strategies, you will find yourself winning the game more often. Remember, your job as the salesperson is to be constantly closing until you receive the answer that you want. If one attempt doesn't work, simply elicit the objection, overcome it, and move back in for the close. Sometimes you will hear "no" several times before hearing "yes". It's important to stay persistent in the persuasion process, and to keep subtly challenging your clients to take action. The strategies outlined in this chapter work, and they have helped me sell myself and my services since I was 19 years old. When you master these techniques, you will be hearing "YES" again and again in your life. My intention in this chapter was to provide you with some of the most effective techniques in closing the sale. I hope that this chapter piqued your mind enough that you will want to go out and learn many more effective selling strategies. Always remember: sales is a game, so play the game to win.

CHAPTER 9
THE ULTIMATE SALESFORCE

How would you like to have a salesforce that works around the clock promoting your services, constantly driving business to your office, and best of all, they work for free? To what height could your business grow if you had this type of resource at your fingertips? This chapter is devoted to teaching you how to build the most dynamic salesforce in the world. It's going to teach you how to utilize your best assets to dramatically increase your sales. Best of all, accomplishing this task requires absolutely no money. The salesforce I am talking about consists of all your previous clients, and the way to get them on your team is by building strong relationships with them. My good friend, Tom Nicoli, told me on several occasions that in order to succeed in any business, it's all about people, and building relationships is the key to success. Anything that you don't have now you will get from another person, and that's why learning to create great relationships with others is the key to success. This chapter is going to break down the importance of building solid relationships with your clients, as well as give examples of simple strategies that you can implement to increase the success of your practice. Let's jump in now and discover how to turn your clients into the best salesforce in the world.

In the game of sales, ineffective salespeople think the game is over once you close the sale. The truth is, when you close the sale, it's just the beginning. It's important to know that the process of selling is like building rapport: it's a never-ending process and not a static state. Once you have closed the sale, your efforts need to shift towards finding ways to keep this client coming back and wanting more. So what is it that causes people to stay loyal to a company and do business with them year in and year out? It is achieved by taking the time to build solid relationships with your clients and consistently showing them that you care. When you produce success with your clients and take the time to make your clients feel that they are important and not just another client, then your salesforce is on the rise. My father always told me, "Make your clients raving fans, because when you do, they will spread the word." This fact is a vital one to remember, because in this business the majority of your work will come through word-of-mouth marketing. When you have people in your fan club, there is no doubt your business will grow.

In my opinion, there are two areas that you need to focus on in order to get people to enroll in your fan club and become promoters of your services. These two areas are competency and character (or in this case, CAREacter, as my father says).

Competency is expected when your clients book a session with you. Your first job as a new hypnotist is to develop your skills enough to deliver a powerful breakthrough session with your clients. Results are a must if you want to generate business through referrals and past clients. However, results by themselves are not enough. You must find a way to separate yourself from other hypnotists. During my conversations with my father, he would ask me questions like, "What is the difference between a party and a party?" In other words, what is going to be the difference between you and the hypnotist down the road? What are you going to do to create the "WOW factor," so that when a client leaves your office they can't help but tell others about their experience? The WOW factor is what makes people want to come back again and again. So how do you develop the WOW factor with your clients? The answer to this question can be found in your own creative mind, and it can be discovered by asking yourself questions like this: What can I do to be different from other hypnotists? How can I make this session memorable? What can I do to enhance what's already being done? How can I make my session unique?

By asking questions like these, the creative function in your mind will begin to generate answers for you. Write down all of your ideas and evaluate ways to make them a reality in your sessions.

Here are a few other suggestions for ways that you can create the WOW factor in your sessions. First, under-promise and over-deliver or, in other words, fulfill all that you say you will and then some. Next, you must deliver a powerful breakthrough session that meets the client's expectations. This is achieved by using modern hypnotic techniques that validate to people that they were in fact hypnotized. It is my opinion that the easiest way to deliver the WOW factor is to stop using outdated methods like the progressive relaxation (if it doesn't include testing) and use induction methods like the Elman, Hand to Face, or Rapid Induction followed by some sort of testing of the state. Testing, especially in the first session, has to be a must because this is what helps the client know that there is no doubt that they were hypnotized. Don't be naïve and think that all hypnotists deliver in this way. There are many hypnotists who are using outdated methods with no convincers, which helps the rest of us, because we steal away all their business by providing sessions that meet clients' expectations. Always remember that people are coming to be hypnotized and they want to know they were, so always make sure to use convincers in your sessions and your clients will always leave satisfied. Finally, use advanced techniques in your sessions like age regression, parts therapy, timeline work, and so on to help your clients create rapid breakthroughs. Direct suggestions are a powerful way to create change, and when they are combined with advanced techniques you will dramatically increase your success rate. Plus, by developing your skills in using advanced techniques, you will definitely separate yourself from the hypnotists who are just using direct suggestion scripts. Just like with your business, constantly ask yourself, "How can I be different? How can I do this better? And what can I do to leave a lasting impression?" Competency is expected, but excellence is going beyond the client's expectations and delivering the WOW factor.

To get people enrolled in your salesforce, you must be more than just competent as a hypnotist. You must have *CAREacter*. *CAREacter* means doing the little things that go above and beyond to let the client know that you care. It's very important to make all of your clients feel special and not like just another client. It is so easy to do this, and the strategies outlined in this section are so simple, yet most people don't put in the extra effort to do these things. The simplest way to show *CAREacter* is by sending your clients a thank you note after the session is over.

This easy task is often overlooked by many people, but it is something that leaves a major impression in the minds of your clients.A thank you note lets the client know that you appreciate their business, shows them that you care, and lets them know you value their success and happiness. Now that e-mail is the most accepted way of receiving mail, thank you notes don't cost you a thing, just 5 minutes of your time. Make sending a thank you note a part of your routine when you work with your clients. As soon as they leave, sit down at your computer and send them a thank you e-mail. You can save even more time by creating a generic e-mail, and then add a customized line to personalize it to your client. Thank you notes are one of the simplest things you can do and also one of the most powerful ways to keep clients coming back to work with you.

Besides a thank you e-mail, I believe a follow-up call is absolutely mandatory. This action truly lets the client know you care about them. Early on in my career, I never did follow-up calls, and ended up missing out on a lot of business. I believe that there are many hypnotists out there who were like me and didn't make follow-up calls a few days after the session. In fact, I know this to be true in my area, because the majority of my clients tell me I'm the only one who has taken the time to give them a call to see how they are doing. Looking back on the beginning of my career, I think I was afraid to get the news that the session wasn't a success, and therefore I rarely made follow-up calls to my clients. I figured if they didn't contact me, then everything was going great, and if they needed more help they would call me. Several months into my career, I quickly learned that this post session strategy wasn't the most effective way to generate more business and build relationships with my clients. I used self-hypnosis to push past my fears, and I discovered that the follow-up call is one of the most important things we can do for our business.

The follow-up call is a vital thing to do for several reasons. First of all, the call lets the client know you care. This simple action makes your clients feel important and special, since you took the time to give them a quick call. Second, it makes you stand out and delivers the WOW factor. It is so rare to hear from a doctor, a dentist, or another professional after an appointment, that when a client gets a call from you, it leaves a lasting impression on their mind. Next, you get to hear about all of the success you helped to create so far in your client's life. It's great to find out about their success, because it will boost your confidence in your talents and make you feel great since you were able to be of service. When you get a happy and satisfied client on the phone, you need to do three things. First, ask them to write up a small testimonial as an inspiration to other clients. Testimonials are worth their weight in gold since they are invaluable for future marketing. Next, ask your client if they know of a few friends who would be interested in achieving the same success, and get their contact information (i.e. phone number or e-mail). Finally, be sure to ask them what else you can help them with. Work on getting the client to address more issues, or set up a session in the future for reinforcement.

The final reason for doing a follow-up call is to discover if the client has been experiencing challenges. I used to be afraid of hearing news that wasn't 100% successful, however now I know that this is an opportunity in the making. As a hypnotist, you should know that hypnosis is a therapeutic process and not a magic bullet. Your clients don't have to change their entire life in one or two sessions, and in order for long term behavioral change to take place, your clients need reinforcement and encouragement of the changes. So when your clients report news that they need more work, you must immediately reframe the situation from a failure to a learning experience. It's important to discover what works for the client and what needs to be adjusted. You must let your clients know that this is a process, and that it can take a few sessions for all changes to be integrated into their daily lives. I let my clients know that even though they didn't achieve what they wanted right away, the session was still a success since we know now that we need to take a different route to achieve the goal. This step opens the door to booking the client again, which generates more business and helps your client get closer to reaching his or her goals.

Sometimes the client has achieved tremendous success, but they believe they have failed when all they really need is another session or two. For example, say you were working with a two-pack-a-day smoker, and when you do your follow-up call a few days later they report they have smoked five cigarettes a day since the session. Many people in this situation feel like they were unsuccessful, and it is your job to reframe this situation to show the client the success he or she actually achieved. This person went from their typical 120 cigarettes over three days down to 15 cigarettes total; that is significant success. You must let the client know how great he or she did and inform him or her that some people need a few more sessions to succeed completely. Let your client know that everyone makes changes at their own pace, so your client should come back in and continue his or her progress. The likelihood of he or she coming back in is very high, especially since you took the time to give the client a call and let him or her know you care about them. There are many benefits to spending five minutes to give your clients a follow-up call. No matter what information comes up during the call, reframe it to indicate success, and utilize it to close the client on more sessions (or reinforcement products).

It is also a good idea to do follow-up calls repeatedly throughout the course of the year. This will provide you with accurate information about client results and enable you to produce statistics about your services. Follow-up calls will help you to build solid relationships with your clients, which will generate continuous business due to top of mind awareness.

TOP OF THE MIND AWARENESS is the goal of all businesses and entrepreneurs, and should be a concept that you always run your business by. Marketing specialists have said that a person must see your name or be exposed to your business at least 7-10 times before they will take action on your services or product. Top of mind awareness means getting your name exposed to the public and to your clients as often as possible. If you are constantly displaying your name in front of people, they are more likely to take action. The goal is to make your name synonymous with your industry, so that when hypnosis comes up in conversation, you are the first person they think of. Follow-up calls throughout the year help to achieve top of mind awareness with your previous clients. It lets them know you care while at the same time forcing them to think about their experience again, which they typically will go talk about with someone. You can also use this opportunity to tell them about upcoming events or programs which they might find interesting.

Another way to achieve top of mind awareness is through e-mails. E-mails are an excellent way to keep your clients and potential clients informed of all the activities going on at your practice, as well as discounts or promotions you may be offering. It is very important to get people's e-mail addresses, because when you generate a significant e-mail list, it will bring in business for years to come. This is the easiest and most efficient way to achieve top of mind awareness, and there are many e-mail services available to make this process simple and effortless.

Other online services that are valuable in showing your clients you care are e-card services. There are companies that let you enter people's birthdays and anniversaries into a generated e-card which is then sent to your client on the day of the event. This is a very easy way to let a person know that they are not just another client, but that you truly care about them. If you decide to use a service like this, make the anniversary date the day of their first session or the day they achieved success (i.e. became a non-smoker). Also, be sure to include a coupon or something free as a birthday gift or anniversary present. This is a surefire way to generate top of mind awareness and many more referrals.

Your goal in building solid relationships is to generate a constant stream of referrals from your salesforce. How do you get these referrals? You get referrals from doing all of the above, and you also get them by asking for them. It is OK to ask your clients directly for referrals, and, in my opinion the best time to do this is after a successful session. When your clients are in ecstasy after the session, you are given the opportunity to suggest that they take some of your business cards to give out to their family and friends. You can also be more direct and simply hand them a small stack to give out. This way, when they are telling their friends about the great experience they had in your office, they will have your cards ready to give to them. Always keep in mind that your clients are sometimes the guinea pig for the group, and when they have a successful experience, there are typically others who will be calling you shortly after. So make sure your clients have cards and brochures to give out to their friends and families.

It is also a great idea to ask for a list of referrals when you do your follow-up calls. Ask your clients who they know that is interested in achieving the same success. Also, inform them that their friends can join your mailing list to stay updated about events and discounts. Finally, ask your successful clients for their doctor's number and ask them if it's OK to inform him or her of their success. If your client was there for smoking, weight reduction, or stress management and had successful results, call their doctor's office and inform them of the news. Then ask the secretary or doctor if it would be OK to send some brochures and cards to give to their patients who need to produce similar results. By approaching a doctor's office from the outside in, you stand a better chance of getting them to become steady supporters of your services. Also, be sure to send the doctor a thank you note and perks from time to time as an appreciation for sending you business. It's important to let everyone know that you are grateful for their business, especially if they are sending you more clients.

These are just a few ways to build solid relationships, generate ongoing business, and create a salesforce that's constantly sending you referrals. The rest is now up to you. It's important to think of other ways to make you stand out and create the WOW factor for your clients. Here are a series of questions that you can ask yourself so that you can come up with some unique ideas that let your clients know you care about them. You will also be able to think of ways to keep your services on the top of your clients' minds.

In what ways can I let my clients know that I care?
How can I make myself stand out next to the competition?
How would I like to be treated if I were a client?
What are some ways that I can create top of the mind awareness?
How can I be more unique?
How can I creatively generate referrals?
How do I turn my clients into a salesforce?
How can I use the web to keep my clients informed?

These types of questions will help you discover more ways to create clients for life. When you take the time to show people you care, they will help you by spreading the word. Take care of your clients, and you will always have more than enough business. Be sure to remember the advice of my friend Tom Nicoli: "It's all about people."

CHAPTER 10
THE FINAL ELEMENTS

Now that you know a variety of strategies for selling your services, the final elements that need to be implemented in order to succeed are passion and action. In the game of sales, these two elements will be the elements that will determine your level of success. Let's finish up this crash course on selling by examining these two final elements of the process.

My father has told me throughout the years that when you light yourself on fire, people will come to watch you burn. What he means is, when you live your life full of passion, people will flock to you because they will want what you have. Passion is an essential element in growing your practice as well as selling your services. When you have passion for what you do, your enthusiasm will rub off on your clients, and they too will get excited about what you are offering. Going back to the idea that all sales start with you, if you believe in what you are offering and present it with passion, people will gravitate towards you. Passion is a rare thing these days, and the people who are bold enough to express it are the ones who get ahead in life. Hypnosis is a service that is so easy to get excited about. We are able to help many people achieve amazing results, and this modality is the vehicle that creates major breakthroughs. If you can't get passionate about this, then you are in the wrong industry. Let your excitement shine through in everything you do, especially when you talk to anybody about your work. Your passion may be just the thing to finally get a client to take action.

Here are some daily questions that you can ask yourself in order to build the passion inside of you. It is good to ask yourself these questions in the morning, before a session, or before a sales call. Be sure that you not only answer the question, but that you allow yourself to feel the feelings you are eliciting.

What about my business gets me excited?

What do I love about my work?

What am I proud about in my work?

What will I do exciting today?

What excites me about my business?

Why do I want to succeed?

What do I love about helping clients?

What excites me about this client today?

What interesting new thing will I do in session today?

How can I make my work fun today?

Ask yourself questions like these every day, and set yourself up for success. These questions will get your energy flowing and your passion levels rising. When you light yourself on fire, people will come to watch you burn!

Taking action is the next crucial element in selling yourself. Knowledge is not power; it is only potential power that comes alive when it's combined with action. In order for this new information to benefit you, you must take action on these new ideas every day. Show the world your level of commitment by taking consistent action rather than just talking. Talking produces reasons, but only actions produce results. Below are a series of questions that will encourage you to take action. Ask yourself these questions every day, and immediately begin taking action on the answers that come to you. When you do, you will never be at a loss for what to do next.

What is one thing I can do today that is outside my comfort zone?
What is one thing I can do that will challenge me today?
What is the most difficult task of the day for me?
How am I going to get my name out to the public today?
How can I use the Internet to better sell my services?
Who can I call today to book a big sale?

Make sure that you write down your answers and use them to develop an action plan for your day, week, or month. Sometimes when you ask yourself questions like these, your mind might answer: "I don't know." When this happens to you or you get this response from your clients, immediately ask this question: "I know you don't know, but if you did know, what would you do?" I know this question seems a little odd at first, but it will produce an answer to the question. As soon as an answer comes to mind, you have figured it out. This question works because it gives the mind permission to be wrong and still produce an answer, as well as paces the mind or the client by stating: "I know you don't know."

Another strategy that has helped me take steps that really moved me forward was asking myself these two questions: "What is the one thing I really don't want to do today?" and "What is the one thing that I would love to put off today?" As soon as I get my answer, I know what task needs to be completed first and right away. The easiest way for a person to get ahead in their business is by starting with the most difficult tasks first, and then progressing to the easiest. However, most ineffective people start with the simplest thing and work towards the hardest. This strategy keeps a person busy, but busy doing the wrong things. Be productive by tackling the tough things first, because when you do you will have more free time, less stress, and be able to make big strides in growing your business.

When you live your life with passion and take consistent action, it is inevitable that your business and life will soar to new levels of success. You have unique talents and gifts inside of you. Be confident in yourself and dare to be bold enough to let your passion radiate in everything that you do, especially when it comes to hypnosis. You will find your energy to be contagious, and when you combine it with consistent actions that are geared towards your achieving your goals, there will be nothing that can stop you from success. Always remember: to succeed you need passion and action.

CHAPTER 11
CONCLUSION

You have just undergone a crash course in selling hypnosis. Throughout this book, you learned about the two truths in the hypnosis profession, which are:

1. You will always have two roles to fulfill; the helper and the entrepreneur.
2. It is perfectly acceptable to make a lot of money in a helping profession.

We reviewed congruity, and how all sales start with you. You have learned techniques such as mirroring and matching in order to build rapport instantly, and strategies to maintain it throughout the relationship. The telephone call was broken down, and you now know the best way to answer the phone, ways to keep the conversation going, how to classify your caller, and what the ultimate goal of every phone call should be. You learned about the importance of selling value, and how when this is done successfully, it is very easy to close any client. You know now how to use objections to your advantage by pacing the objection and turning it back into a closing attempt. We broke down several easy, yet very effective ways to close the sale. You learned about using the Scale of Readiness, the Either or Assumption close, the Pro/Con close, and other strategies that will help to increase your success. We discussed the importance of building solid relationships as a way to grow your business through top of the mind awareness. Finally, the last essential elements, passion and action, were reinforced, as were ways to implement these two elements in your everyday life.

You now possess a concrete foundation in the world of selling hypnosis, and my hope is that this book will inspire you to learn more about this fascinating field. Hypnosis and sales are very closely linked, and I highly recommend that you make it a goal to continue to read about and develop your knowledge of these areas. When you do, you will find new ways to utilize these techniques in both the persuasion process and hypnosis.

Let me take this opportunity to praise you for being a hypnotist who is committed to excellence. I wholeheartedly believe in you, and know that you can achieve all that you desire. With these tools, you are truly on the road to becoming a master persuader and an unstoppable salesperson. Live your life with passion and take consistent action, and as you do, you will watch your dreams become your new reality. Now go out there and produce the results you deserve.

A Word about the Resources of
The National Guild of Hypnotists

The Guild is a not-for-profit, educational corporation in the State of New Hampshire. Founded in Boston, Massachusetts in 1950/51, it is a professional organization comprised of more than 10,000 dedicated hypnotists (from 65 countries) committed to advancing the field of hypnotism. The Guild is a resource for members and a vehicle for legal and legislative action.

Dr. Rexford L. North, Director of the Hypnotism Center of Boston, founded the Guild in 1950/51. Within a short time, local chapters were formed and operating in many major cities throughout the US and Canada. Important resources through the years have been two publications devoted exclusively to the field of hypnotism: *The Journal of Hypnotism* and *The HypnoGram*.

This unique organization encourages an eclectic exchange of ideas, fellowship, mutual trust and cooperation among members—while promoting and protecting the science, art, and philosophy of hypnotism. Dr. Dwight F. Damon, the President of the National Guild of Hypnotists, has made a personal commitment to have the practice of hypnotism recognized as a separate and distinct profession. The National Guild of Hypnotists is fair-minded and has always assisted wherever needed, helping other groups and individuals regardless of their affiliations.

Each year in August the National Guild of Hypnotists holds the world's largest annual hypnosis educational conference and convention. Hypnotists from all over the world attend this event.

For more information contact:
The National Guild of Hypnotists
P.O. Box 308
Merrimack, NH 03054-0308
(603) 429-9438 (FAX) 424-8066
NGH e-mail address: ngh@ngh.net
NGH Web Page: http://www.ngh.net

www.ingramcontent.com/pod-product-compliance
Lightning Source LLC
Chambersburg PA
CBHW060557100426

42742CB00013B/2589